Flip, Spin & Play

Creating Interactive Scrapbook Pages

FROM THE EDITORS OF MEMORY MAKERS BOOKS

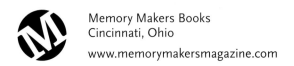

Memory Makers Books
Cincinnati, Ohio

www.memorymakersmagazine.com

Flip, Spin & Play. Copyright © 2007 by Memory Makers Books. Printed in China.
All rights reserved. It is permissible for the purchaser to make the projects contained herein and sell
them at fairs, bazaars and craft shows. No other part of this book may be reproduced in any form or
by any electronic or mechanical means including information storage and retrieval systems without
permission in writing from the publisher, except by a reviewer, who may quote a brief passage in review.
Published by Memory Makers Books, an imprint of F+W Publications, Inc., 4700 East Galbraith Road,
Cincinnati, Ohio 45236. (800) 289-0963. First edition.

11 10 09 08 07   5 4 3 2 1

Distributed in Canada by Fraser Direct
100 Armstrong Avenue
Georgetown, ON, Canada L7G 5S4
Tel: (905) 877-4411

Distributed in the U.K. and Europe by David & Charles
Brunel House, Newton Abbot, Devon, TQ12 4PU, England
Tel: (+44) 1626 323200, Fax: (+44) 1626 323319
E-mail: postmaster@davidandcharles.co.uk

Distributed in Australia by Capricorn Link
P.O. Box 704, S. Windsor, NSW 2756 Australia
Tel: (02) 4577-3555

Library of Congress Cataloging-in-Publication Data
Flip, spin & play : creating interactive scrapbook pages / editors of Memory Makers Books. -- Ist ed.
    p. cm.
  Includes index.
  ISBN-13: 978-1-59963-018-2 (pbk. : alk. paper)
 1. Photograph albums. 2. Photographs--Conservation and restoration. 3. Scrapbooks. I. Memory
Makers Books.
TR465.F65 2007
745.593--dc22

                                        2007022313

EDITOR:
AMY GLANDER

DESIGNER:
JEREMY WERLING

ART COORDINATOR:
EILEEN ABER

PRODUCTION COORDINATOR:
MATT WAGNER

PHOTOGRAPHERS:
CHRISTINE POLOMSKY;
TIM GRONDIN; JOHN CARRICO,
ADAM HENRY, ADAM LEIGH-
MANUELL, ALIAS IMAGING LLC

STYLIST:
JAN NICKUM

WRITER:
TORREY SCOTT

Metric Conversion Chart

TO CONVERT	TO	MULTIPLY BY
Inches	Centimeters	2.54
Centimeters	Inches	0.4
Feet	Centimeters	30.5
Centimeters	Feet	0.03
Yards	Meters	0.9
Meters	Yards	1.1
Sq. Inches	Sq. Centimeters	6.45
Sq. Centimeters	Sq. Inches	0.16
Sq. Feet	Sq. Meters	0.09
Sq. Meters	Sq. Feet	10.8
Sq. Yards	Sq. Meters	0.8
Sq. Meters	Sq. Yards	1.2
Pounds	Kilograms	0.45
Kilograms	Pounds	2.2
Ounces	Grams	28.3
Grams	Ounces	0.035

fw
F+W PUBLICATIONS, INC.
www.fwbookstore.com

Contributing Artists

Jodi Amidei

Vicki Boutin

Karen Burniston

Alecia Grimm

Greta Hammond

Linda Harrison

Becky Heisler

Nic Howard

Caroline Ikeji

Jen Lowe

Kelli Noto

Suzy Plantamura

Torrey Scott

Samantha Walker

Courtney Walsh

Amanda Williams

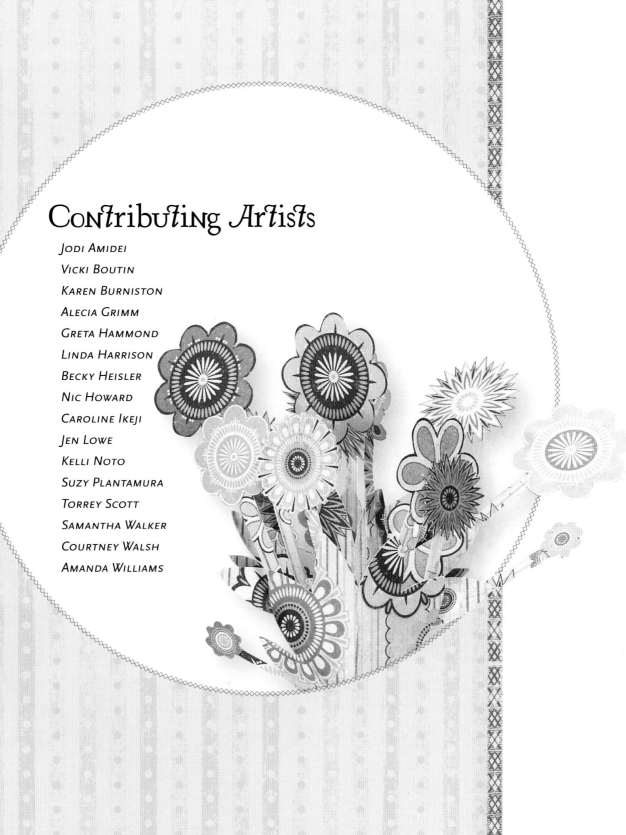

laugh

your face lights up as
your WhoLE BoDy
ErUpTS with laughter

Just the 2 of Us

somersaults

enjoying the QUIeT times

There are a list of things I could tell you about why I love summer. I regularly create layouts showing how much we love to take off to the beach for holidays, how we love the freedom and fun of getting 'away from it all', just how much we love to watch the kids totally relax and just enjoy nature provides. What you don't see me talking about much though, is how much I love that we can make the outside part of our home. Those parts of summer when we get up in the morning and can open all the doors and windows and the kids freely in and out all day. When it is so hot the kids play in the sprinkler, which I place under the trampoline. We hang outside, in the small patches of shade we can find, hoping to find a cool breeze. These pictures of Abby & I were taken on of those days. I was just sitting out on the deck, watching the kids play. Abby was just hanging out playing beside me. these are the things about summer I love.

January 2007

Table Of Contents

7   Introduction

8   **1**   Touchable Textures

32   **2**   To Slide or Not To Slide

64   **3**   The Skinny on Spinning & Flipping

96   **4**   A Passion for Pop-Ups

120   Templates

125   Source Guide

127   Index

Introduction

For years, the focus on scrapbooking has been geared almost exclusively toward the visual. This may have been the standard when scrapbooking was in its infancy...but now scrapbooking is all grown-up and ready to spread its creative wings and take flight! There's nothing wrong with layouts that are safely bound in page protectors—like works of art displayed at a museum. But for those scrapbookers who crave more, we say "MOVE OVER!" to those conventional layouts. The eyes have had their turn. Now it's time to give the rest of the senses some much-needed play time. Interactive scrapbooking is so much fun—and it's addictive, too. Before you know it, you'll be including interactive elements in all your projects. HOORAY!

Are you intimidated by adding interactive features to your layouts? Don't know where to start or how? Are you simply at the "There-is-no-way-I-could-ever-do-this" stage? Have a little faith in that creative muse who lives within you. Let's turn the pages together as we explore elements that flip, spin, pop up, slide, pull out, and some really fun textural ways to bring your scrapbooking to life and launch it into the new millennium.

LEVEL OF DIFFICULTY
As you browse through the book, you will see we have noted the level of complexity as it relates to the interactive technique displayed in the overall project. The projects themselves run the gamut from quick-and-easy to over-the-top.

● SIMPLE ● ● INTERMEDIATE ● ● ● ADVANCED

CHAPTER 1

Touchable Textures

In scrapbooking we start with the photos. In a symphony, the photos would be the melody line. They are a great foundation, but by themselves, photos are just fragments of a memory. Back to the symphony analogy—so if photos are the melody, what is the harmony? Texture, that's what. Texture adds depth and breadth to our layouts. It breathes life into what could be a mundane existence for our precious memories. Whether it's rough, smooth, scratchy, soft, silky, slippery or gritty, texture is what flavors our layouts with vibrant richness. Whether you're a lumpy, bumpy scrapbooker, or one who likes subtlety when it comes to texture, we've got it all here to share and inspire you. It's time to get up-close and personal with scrapbooking. Pull off the white gloves and let your fingers do the walking...don't be afraid to get touchy-feely. When it comes to scrapbooking, it's just another way to bring those wonderful memories to life.

Baby Steps

Many scrapbookers have a fear of lumpiness when it comes to their layouts. They fear their pages won't fit in their protectors and the texture will splay the pages of the album apart so it won't close. These are valid concerns, but it is totally possible to add the illusion of dimensionality with minimally added "loft" to your page. Try taking a few die cuts and using a thin foam spacer to gently lift it off the background of the layout. Even 1/8" (3mm) can give the illusion of great depth! Remember, you don't have to go lumpy to add dimension. Take baby steps!

ART CREATED BY AMANDA WILLIAMS

A Little Dab Will Do

Make a splash with textured-cardstock page elements! It's quick and easy to add texture to otherwise plain Jane cardstock. On this layout, Linda used three sizes of circular embossing templates to create rings in the light blue cardstock background. She added further texture by embossing a daisy pattern on the border and title letters with an embossing die and die-cut machine. The possibilities are endless! From embossing dies and punches, to styluses, templates and stencils...all it takes is a few tools, a light box and some elbow grease and you can texturize just about anything. Don't be afraid to experiment with household objects and other found treasures to emboss into your cardstock.

ART CREATED BY LINDA HARRISON

Supplies: *Cardstock; patterned paper (Imagination Project); plastic letters (Heidi Swapp); die-cut letters, flower embossing die (QuicKutz); embossing templates (Lasting Impressions); corner rounder; Traveling Typewriter font (Internet download)*

I definitely lost count as to how many times we played water balloons this past summer. Each time sure was fun, though!

Summer 2006

Totally Tulle

Fabric stores are a great place to find all sorts of interesting things to add texture to your layouts. The nice thing is, most sewing notions and fabrics are completely safe to use in scrapbooking (just steer clear of vinyl and faux leather). Tulle is a wonderful choice for adding texture to your projects without adding bulk, and without emptying your wallet! It comes in fun colors, and if you don't find the color you want...no sweat! Just dye it with dye-based stamp pads to achieve the color you desire. Follow along and we'll show you how easy it can be to use tulle in your next project.

ART CREATED BY CAROLINE IKEJI

Supplies: *Cardstock; patterned paper (KI Memories); letter stickers (American Crafts, Heidi Swapp); digital frames and stars (Designer Digitals); buttons; tulle; floss; pen*

Trim strips of tulle in various colors.

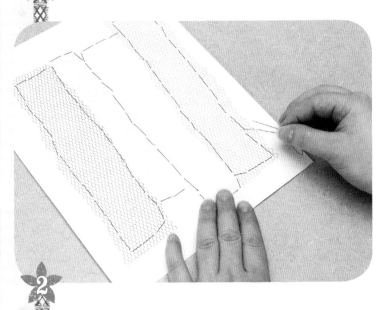

Layer and hand stitch the tulle to your page background using a needle and embroidery floss. To finish, adhere your photos and embellishments over the tulle.

Flip It Tip

Here's a list of memorabilia to touch and feel. These items are well-suited for a hands-on layout:

Sand from a beach (adhere with glue for a rough texture)
Pieces of sea glass (house in a memory keeper)
Fabric from a favorite garment or cherished baby blanket
Grandmother's buttons
Lock of hair
Price tags from new clothing
Costume jewelry
Old letters

Supplies: *Chipboard heart, stars and word, patterned paper (Fancy Pants); letter stickers (EK Success); felt flowers (American Crafts); die-cut flowers (Provo Craft); buttons (Autumn Leaves); acrylic paint; stamping ink; thread*

Warm and Fuzzy

There's just something so soft and cuddly about the spontaneous, unbridled laughter of a child. What better way to illustrate this than by including soft and cuddly textures on your layout? At least we've always "felt" that way. So grab those bits and pieces and odds and ends of felt lurking in your supply caché and cut them into interesting shapes to use as embellishments for just about any theme. For added texture, sew a few quick stitches with embroidery thread and some brightly colored buttons. Your layout will be giggling in no time.

ART CREATED BY GRETA HAMMOND

Rustic Appeal

There is something very alluring about primitive, rustic elements. They speak to a time when life was slower, less-complicated, more "real." The elements of this layout lend a feeling of time-worn warmth and infuse the layout with a folksy feeling of handmade goodness. Bits of fabric, haphazard stitching, uneven strips of paper and buttons come together to give this layout an air of soft-spoken dignity and charm. It's rough around the edges—just as it should be.

ART CREATED BY BECKY HEISLER

Supplies: *Patterned paper (BasicGrey); rub-on letters and accents (7gypsies, Autumn Leaves); buttons (Autumn Leaves, Buttons Galore); fabric (unknown); floss; thread; pen*

It was always strange to me when you were a baby and people would make the comment "He's a REAL boy" or "He just looks like a little boy!" I always thought, 'He is a boy! What else is he going to look like?' But more and more as you grow, I think I understand what they were trying to say. That there are times that you just look so much more in your boyish element. Times that you look so content, so masculine, so rough and so in your own.

I guess there are a few times when you don't appear this way as much, but for the most part, you sure do have that authentic boyish appeal that is definitely noticed, and especially loved.

Robby 2006

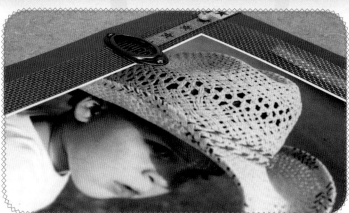

Supplies: *Cardstock; brads, charm, rub-on and sticker accents (Bo-Bunny); bookplate, metal trim (Making Memories); wire mesh, metal photo corner (unknown); adhesive foam; Maiandra GD font (Internet download)*

Pedal To The Metal

When you are struggling to incorporate textures that truly reflect the rough-and-tumble feeling of that special little (or big) guy, it's time to head to the hardware store. Yep. The hardware store is a fabulous place to find all sorts of interesting metal doodads to turn into scrapbooking embellishments. But whether you get them from a hardware store or from your local craft or scrapbooking store, metal accents can lend just the right touch of texture while maintaining a totally masculine feel.

ART CREATED BY LINDA HARRISON

Rough and Tumble

Snips and snails and puppy dog tails (or so the adage reads). For a little boy, when it comes to play, a little dirt is all he needs! Ripped jeans, dirty socks, sand in the shoes. Yep, that's what being a boy is all about. Soft and frilly things don't apply here. To capture the essence of boyhood, subtlety just won't cut it. Corrugated cardboard, denim, metal and digital distressing add just the right amount of boyish charm.

ART CREATED BY GRETA HAMMOND

Supplies: *Cardstock; chipboard letters, patterned paper (Imagination Project); letter stickers (EK Success); digital frame (Two Peas in a Bucket); brads, fabric tags (Making Memories); stamping ink; thread*

Digging in the make-shift sand pile. Pushing the sand around and playing with rusty old tractors.

Making noises and sound effects to go with every movement. Intently blazing new trails and piles. Unaware of everyone and everything around you.

Using your imagination and getting caught up in your own world. Doing what boys do.

Supplies: *Cardstock; patterned paper (BasicGrey, CherryArte, Urban Lily); chipboard letters (Scenic Route); ribbon, rub-on stitching (American Crafts); fabric (unknown); thread; pen*

Layers of Texture

There are as many ways to add texture to a layout as there are moods of a toddler—perhaps even more. This layout incorporates a veritable smorgasbord of different textural elements. Machine stitching, paper piercing, ribbon, fabric, sanding, paper layering, clear lacquer, chipboard elements...the list goes on and on. Don't feel like you're limited to using just one or two textural elements. Pile them on, layer after layer, to create a layout that's rich and full.

ART CREATED BY BECKY HEISLER

Subtle Textures

You don't have to put chunks of tree bark and rocks on your layout to give it texture (though we know scrapbookers who have done that). Even the addition of subtle textures can add an amazing amount of depth. There are so many products available today to bring "feeling" to your layout. Combine flocked papers with dry-embossed pieces of cardstock to turn up the volume on your layout. It's an easy, breezy, beautiful way to sass up a page.

ART CREATED BY VICKI BOUTIN

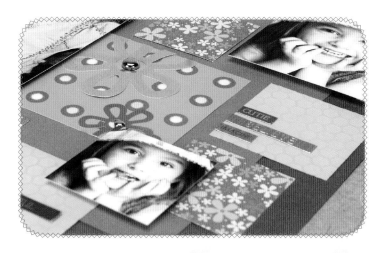

Supplies: *Cardstock; flowers, metal and traditional word stickers, patterned paper (Heidi Grace); brads; stamping ink; texture plate (Fiskars); pen*

Supplies: *Cardstock; chipboard letters (Heidi Swapp); letter stickers (Making Memories); chipboard accent (Fancy Pants); ribbon (Chatterbox, May Arts, Michaels, Offray); conchos (Scrapworks); adhesive foam; pen*

Ribbons, Ribbons Everywhere

The background of this bright and cheery layout may look like patterned paper, but it's not! The entire background is made from cardstock covered in ribbons—grosgrain, satin, rickrack, gingham, and even stitched. With so many ribbons available on the market today, it's hard to choose just a couple...so why stop at one or two? Stock up! Ribbons make a fabulous foundation to add even more dimension. Metal conchos, photos lifted on foam spacers and chipboard elements complete this layout and make it oh-so touchy-feely.

ART CREATED BY COURTNEY WALSH

Using scissors, trim 12" (30cm) strips of various coordinating ribbons.

Layer and adhere the ribbon over a piece of cardstock to create your page background.

Add photos and embellishments to the page. Use pop-dots on some photos to add dimension.

Flip It Tip

Get touchy-feely! Here's a buffet of textures to add some "spice" to your layouts.

Sewing Notions
Ribbons, fabric, trim, buttons, zippers, netting, buckles, snaps

Hardware Finds
Washers, metal flashing, screen, hinges, the whole hardware department

Nature's Bounty
Seashells, flowers, sand, feathers, leaves, seed pods, dried grasses, small rocks

Found Objects
Jewelry, trinkets, doodads, what-nots, thingamajigs, knick-knacks

Dry Embossing
Emboss by hand or with textured templates or brass stencils

Art Mediums
Modeling paste, spackle, air-dry clay, textured paints

Other Goodies
Brads, eyelets, conchos, studs, staples, clips

Love in Bloom

The wedding took place at the Cathedral of the Immaculate Conception in Denver with a reception following at the Olin Hotel. They were married on May 6, 1961. Mary Jane hired a wedding planner from Daniel's and Fisher's Department Store and the package included an overnight stay at the Olin. A friend made the dress for Mary Jane and another friend made her veil. They honeymooned in Santa Fe and Las Vegas.

Supplies: Cardstock; patterned paper (unknown); die-cut letters (QuicKutz); chalk ink; diamond glaze (JudiKins); transparency; adhesive foam

Beautiful Blossoms

Paper flowers are an elegant addition to any layout. But pre-made paper flowers can get pricey. Fear not! You can make your own in a few simple steps. Cut flowers from patterned paper and layer them on your layout with foam spacers. Gussy them up anyway you like: apply a coat of clear lacquer (as shown here), sprinkle with glitter, add beads, buttons, stitching, chalk, ink...whatever your heart desires to give them your own special touch.

ART CREATED BY KELLI NOTO

Rolling Right Along

Machine stitching on a layout is a fun and easy way to add texture to your layout, but why stop there? One uber-cool technique is to stitch very closely to the edge of a paper piece, wet the outside edge of the piece using your finger, a brush or cotton tip applicator and gently roll the paper with your finger toward the stitching. When the paper dries, the rolled edge hardens and maintains its crumpled texture. Be careful though...this technique is very addicting!

ART CREATED BY NIC HOWARD

Supplies: *Cardstock; chipboard letters, letter stickers, patterned paper (Scenic Route); beads (Queen & Co.); glass finish topcoat (Plaid); solvent ink; corner rounder; thread; pen*

oh my goodness

Is the prospect of a kiss from your sister so bad?

Apparently so. January 2007.

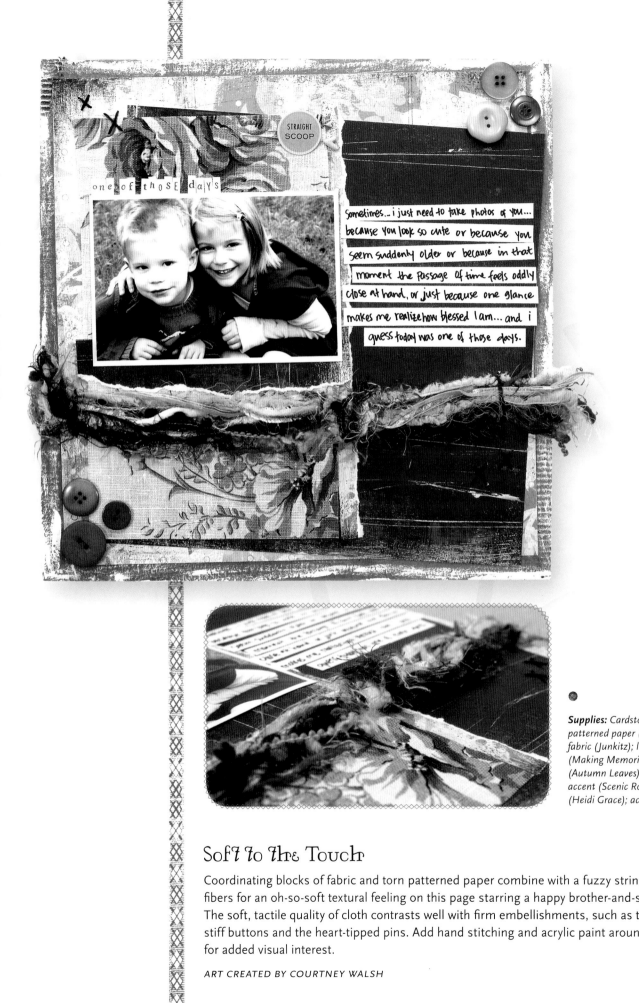

STRAIGHT SCOOP

one of those days

Sometimes... i just need to take photos of you... because you look so cute or because you seem suddenly older or because in that moment the passage of time feels oddly close at hand, or just because one glance makes me realize how blessed I am... and i guess today was one of those days.

Supplies: Cardstock; fibers, patterned paper (BasicGrey); fabric (Junkitz); letter stickers (Making Memories); buttons (Autumn Leaves); floss; sticker accent (Scenic Route); pin (Heidi Grace); acrylic paint; pen

Soft to the Touch

Coordinating blocks of fabric and torn patterned paper combine with a fuzzy string of fibers for an oh-so-soft textural feeling on this page starring a happy brother-and-sister duo. The soft, tactile quality of cloth contrasts well with firm embellishments, such as the smooth, stiff buttons and the heart-tipped pins. Add hand stitching and acrylic paint around the border for added visual interest.

ART CREATED BY COURTNEY WALSH

All That Glitters

Texture is more than something you touch with your fingers. Texture can also be visual. Wake up your projects with sparkly, shiny or glittery elements. They add so much pizzazz to projects. Here, rhinestones frame and enhance the photo beautifully without overwhelming it. Whether you choose sequins, glitter, rhinestones, a mirror, holographic paper or reflective foils, adding a little bling can spice up an otherwise humdrum layout. Go from drab to fab in nothing flat! Bling, baby...it's all about the bling!

ART CREATED BY SUZY PLANTAMURA

Supplies: *Chipboard purse and accents, ribbon, rickrack (Maya Road); cardstock; patterned paper (Collage Press); letter stickers (Making Memories); acrylic paint; glitter; rhinestones (Heidi Swapp, Me & My Big Ideas); rub-on and sticker accents (Creative Imaginations); pen*

A LITTLE BIT EDGY!

WANTED TO BE A FAMOUS ACTRESS

ENGAGED WHEN SHE MET HER HUSBAND

WELL KNOWN FOR HER "SKIT"

NICK NAME WAS "HAIR"

ALWAYS SMILING

HANGS OUT AT A MENTAL HEALTH CLINIC

FAVORITE COLORS- ORANGE, BROWN & BLACK

VOTED MISS PUNK IN MIDDLE SCHOOL

HAS EXERCISED WITH RICHARD SIMMONS

NAMED HER COCKAPOOLESS T-BONE

LOVES HER MAN

ORNERY

SUFFERS FROM ANXIETY

SENDS VICTORIA SECRET UNDIES TO

PEOPLE SHE HAS NEVER MET

LIKES HER BEDROOM WALLS BARE

A WONDERFUL FRIEND

LOVES TO EAT BIG MACS (HUH?!!!)

Photo: Matt Smith

Supplies: *Cardstock; patterned paper (Junkitz, Paper Loft); rub-on letters (Daisy D's); stamps (FontWerks, Technique Tuesday); acrylic paint; embossing powder; metal ribbon slide (7gypsies); photo corners (Heidi Swapp); arrow brad (unknown); solvent and watermark inks; staples; pen*

Urban Grunge

Time to get your grunge on! Take an urban-style layout to the next level with a mixture of daring textural elements. To create a background with a rough finish, combine paint, ink and embossing powder. Stamp title letters with layers of paint and embossing powder for an edgy type treatment. In addition to the tactile texture, this layout is full of visual texture. Use photo-realistic papers and embellishments to add a feeling of texture without ever having to physically touch the layout.

ART CREATED BY SUZY PLANTAMURA

Even The Kitchen Sink

OK, so there isn't a kitchen sink on this layout. But the background is made from a clear, flexible kitchen sink mat. Obtain this unique look by tracing around the "pebbles" in the mat and cutting out pieces of coordinating (or contrasting) patterned paper. Adhere the paper to the back side of each "pebble" and affix the whole assembly to a full sheet of patterned paper to create a truly funkalicious background that just begs to be touched.

ART CREATED BY KAREN BURNISTON

Supplies: *Cardstock; patterned paper (Christine Adolf, Cosmo Cricket, Creative Imaginations); letter stickers (Creative Imaginations); chipboard shapes (Rusty Pickle); brads (Making Memories); ball chain; flowers, ribbon (unknown); transparency; paint; paper crimper; notebook paper; rubber sink mat; pen*

Flip It Tip

Here are some tips for keeping your photos and layouts archival-safe when adding textures, memorabilia or found objects.

Wash and dry hands well before handling layouts

Use pH-neutralizing spray on memorabilia

Place memorabilia in PVC-free plastic pockets

Double mat photos on acid-free cardstock

Laminate paper ephemera

Trim windows in page protectors to allow for easier access to interactive elements

A DOZEN OR SO TIMES A YEAR WE MAKE THE LONG DRIVE TO THE MOUNTAINS

SKI BUM

HE SKIS UNTIL THE LIFTS CLOSE

THEN COMES HOME—BONE WEARY

BUT READY FOR THE NEXT TIME

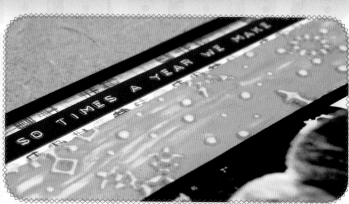

SO TIMES A YEAR WE MAKE

Supplies: *Cardstock; letter stickers, patterned paper, plastic textured sheet (AdornIt); labels (Dymo); acrylic paint; chalk ink*

Texture Plates

Snow: It can take on so many subtle different textures—soft, fluffy, smooth, rough, slick... it's all of these, and more. Texture plates and sheets are a great way to add subtle texture to a winter layout. They are a must-have for any scrapbooker who wants to incorporate a touch of texture in her creations. You can purchase pre-made texture sheets, or create your own texture by using a die-cut machine or a stylus. While Kelli adhered an altered plastic sheet directly to this layout (see step-by-step instructions on the opposite page), the sheets can be used over and over again for dry-embossing cardstock, so they are very cost-effective in the long run.

ART CREATED BY KELLI NOTO

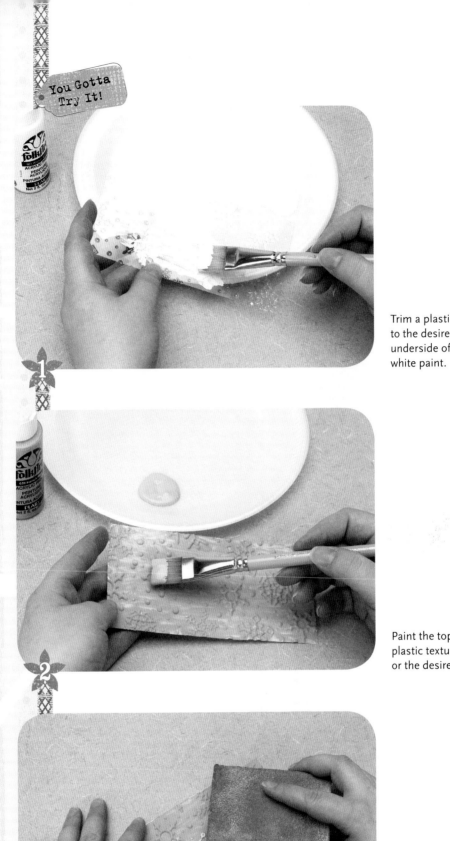

You Gotta Try It!

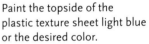

Trim a plastic texture sheet to the desired size. Paint the underside of the plastic with white paint.

Paint the topside of the plastic texture sheet light blue or the desired color.

Sand the paint off the topside of the plastic texture sheet to allow the bottom color of paint to show through. Adhere the plastic sheet to the layout.

Supplies: *Watercolor board (Strathmore); gesso; varnish; walnut ink; modeling paste; ribbon (Offray); denim; chipboard letters and flower (Fancy Pants); metal buttons (unknown); textured paint (Krylon); spray paint*

Blind Ambition

When Samantha completed this project, she said, "I made sure even a blind person could feel what was going on in this layout." It's true. This layout-for-the-wall screams to be touched. From its gesso-covered, tea-dye varnished background, to its border of ribbons and dimensional buttons, this piece of wall art is a feast, not only for the eyes, but for the hands as well. The texture-fest doesn't stop there. Au contraire! Texturized spray paint and modeling paste add even more texture to the chipboard title and flower. Close your eyes and let your fingers do the walking.

ART CREATED BY SAMANTHA WALKER

Bee's Knees

When it comes to adding texture, it's time to explore a more "urban" look. Beeswax is a wonderfully versatile medium that is just finding its way into scrapbooking. It can take on many different appearances. By adding dye, beads, glitter, and even embossing powder, you can devise all sorts of interesting textures. It's just plain fun to experiment with this product. The effect is always different and unique. You can even use it to secure other elements (like this aluminum grating) to your layout. Beeswax—it's all the buzzzz.

ART CREATED BY JODI AMIDEI

Supplies: Cardstock; chipboard letters (K&Co.); wire mesh (unknown); bee's wax (Jacquard); adhesive foam; shelf liner; pen

To Slide or Not to Slide

In our daily lives, we struggle to prevent ourselves from sliding: sliding off diets, sliding off a slippery road while driving, sliding in our responsibilities at work, slipping and sliding on our backsides when we fall down. For this reason, wouldn't it be nice to just go with the flow and let things "slide" so to speak, just once without feeling bad? Thank your lucky stars! Because in scrapbooking, sliding is a GOOD thing. As a matter of fact, you can slide all you want and never feel the least bit of remorse! Make journaling that slides out from behind photos, or tags that slide from their pockets or even dancing elements on your layouts that move when you pull a tab. Creating slides and pulls is just another way to add some interactive spark to your layouts, and we're here to show you how. So give yourself permission to "slide." We know you want to!

Winters can be down right depressing around here. Overcast days are the norm and sometimes it is weeks before we see the sun shine. So when spring finally heads north and sunshine floods through the windows, our spirits are renewed and the world seems to be okay again. That is exactly what happened on this day. We broke out the bright new springy clothes and headed outside, free of hats and gloves. The sunshine warmed our pale skin as well as our souls and smiles were plentiful. There is nothing more invigorating than a warm spring day. And believe me, this one didn't come a day too soon!

April 2006

Supplies: Chipboard letters and shapes, patterned paper, ribbon (Fancy Pants); rub-on flowers and letters (K&Co.); acrylic paint; silk flower (Bazzill); button (Autumn Leaves); floss

Hide & Seek

Large format photos (like the cutie patootie pictured here) are very popular. They're striking, and really add a "wow" factor to your layouts. The problem is, they don't leave much room for anything else. And, as we all know, we (as scrapbookers) are rarely satisfied with putting just one photo on a page. So how do you fit two, three, four or even more pictures on your page? Play hide and seek. When you mat your main photo, leave one entire edge unattached. Then slide a photo (or two or three) behind the main photo. Your viewers are sure to yell, "Olly Olly Oxen Free!" as they discover the photos hidden behind.

ART CREATED BY GRETA HAMMOND

Tab Camouflage

Hiding slide-out journaling is a time-worn staple in interactive elements. The usual method of indicating there is a feature requiring attention is to add a tab that says "pull," or "lift", or whatever action is necessary to reveal it. That little tab can detract from the overall beauty of a layout. Simple solution: disguise your pull tab. Who says a tab has to have a direction written on it? Not us! The tabs for this pull-out journaling look like decorative flower elements and nothing more. The secret is yours.

ART CREATED BY COURTNEY WALSH

Supplies: *Cardstock; patterned paper (created in Adobe); chipboard letters (Heidi Swapp); brads, flowers, photo turns (Queen & Co.); rickrack (unknown); corner rounder; pigment ink; pen*

Flip It Tip

Here are some fun closures and enclosures for interactive flip or slide features:

Zippers

Button/buttonhole

Hooks/eyes

Latches/hasps

Document closure
with string and circles of paper

Photo turns

Clips

Straps and buckles

Ribbon ties

Frogs (Chinese cloth button/loop closures)

Real denim or cloth pockets removed from clothing

Lingerie garters

Jewelry clasps

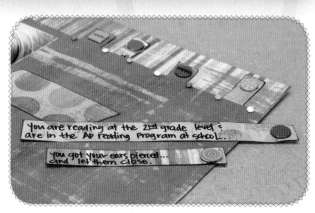

You are reading at the 2nd grade level & are in the AP reading program at school.

You got your ears pierced... and let them close.

Supplies: *Patterned paper (Junkitz); brads, flowers, letters, ribbon pulls (Queen & Co.); ribbon (Chatterbox); pigment ink; pen*

Strip Tease

Got your attention, huh? OK, this isn't a risqué layout—not at all. So it's safe to let the kids back in the room. This layout employs the use of little journaling strips that rest between brads and slide in and out of the background. Aaaaah! Now you get it? You TEASE the journaling STRIPS out of their hiding places by pulling on their handles made from oversized brads. That's the kind of "strip tease" we're talking about. What were YOU thinking?

ART CREATED BY COURTNEY WALSH

Egg-cellent Idea

This little accordion book is eggs-actly the ticket to add more pictures and journaling to your layout! It allows you to include lots of extra photos and journaling without sacrificing any design elements. To make the base for this cute-as-a-bug book, just accordion fold a piece of cardstock several times and cut out your desired shape. Note: Make certain you leave at least a ½" (13mm) piece uncut on both the right and left sides to allow for the accordion action. Then decorate it any way you wish! Don't you think it's time to break out of your shell, and try your hand at a mini accordion book?

ART CREATED BY GRETA HAMMOND

Supplies: *Cardstock; chipboard letters, patterned paper, rub-on letters (Scenic Route); chipboard accents (Fancy Pants, Scenic Route); brads; ribbon (My Mind's Eye)*

Supplies: *Album (American Traditional); cardstock; patterned paper, square letters (Crate Paper); scalloped paper (Creative Imaginations); letter stickers (EK Success, Making Memories, SEI); flowers (Darice, Fancy Pants); buttons (Autumn Leaves); rhinestones; rub-on accents (BasicGrey); stamping ink*

Friendly Fold-Out

This lovely tribute mini-album is reminiscent of the old-fashioned wallet inserts that house snapshots. You know the kind—a proud parent would flip open their wallet and out tumbled an accordion-folded collection of all their kids' photos? This is a take-off on that concept...but people won't go running when this cute album is flipped open! It's an easy yet beautiful way to showcase one person or many. Follow along as we guide you through the process of re-creating pockets for this pretty-as-a-picture album! See template on page 121.

ART CREATED BY AMANDA WILLIAMS

You Gotta Try It!

1 Using a craft knife and a straight-edge ruler, trim double-sided patterned paper into a 4-sided shape (see page 121 for template). Make sure the pattern you want on the exterior of the pocket is facing up when you trim.

2 Fold the left side to the back to form the back of the pocket.

3 Fold the small triangle on the right to the back and secure with adhesive.

4 Print journaling onto cardstock. Trim the cardstock and ink the edges for definition. Add a silk flower with a rhinestone center or other embellishments as desired.

Tag, You're It

Clothes. We all wear them. We all buy them...and they all come with those annoying price tags. But those same tags can certainly make cute and informational embellishments. How fun would it be, years from now, to be able to marvel at how inexpensive clothing was in 2007? One solution is to hang the tags from a hidden journaling file folder that's tucked behind the main photo. Set eyelets along the edge of the folder and at the top of each tag and tie the tags onto the folder with bright ribbon to create a funky and interactive addition.

ART CREATED BY LINDA HARRISON

Supplies: *Cardstock; chipboard letters (Heidi Swapp, unknown); brads, letter stickers, tags (Making Memories); die-cut arrow (Scenic Route); file folder (Junkitz); eyelets; ribbon (Maya Road, Offray); bookplate (KI Memories); stamp (Technique Tuesday); stamping ink; circle punch; floss; adhesive foam*

Expressions

Let's face it, none of us are all sunshiny and smiley all the time. Sometimes we're sad, sometimes angry, sometimes we're even just bored. Here is a fun way to display all those emotions in a blink of an eye! Using several same-size photos of different facial emotions is the key to this clever sliding feature. Cut a window where the mouth would be on the main photo, and place photos of different expressions on a slide-out strip. Pull the strip and watch the mood parade! This would also be a fun technique if you used different facial features from many different people to make fun and silly combinations.

ART CREATED BY CAROLINE IKEJI

Supplies: *Cardstock; patterned paper (American Crafts, KI Memories, Making Memories); chipboard letters (Heidi Swapp); letter stickers, plastic flower (American Crafts); sticker trim (KI Memories); rhinestones (Heidi Swapp, Junkitz); rub-on accents (Hambly); pen*

Slide Into Love

We love our children, that's a given. We love scrapbooking layouts of our children every chance we get. But sometimes, the kids don't like being the subject of all our heartfelt mushy gushy journaling. This is a great place for a compromise. They let us take pictures of them...and we, in turn, will hide away the sappy journaling so they won't be too embarrassed. It's a DEAL! Just create journaling blocks with tabs and slide them behind the photos. In the end everybody's happy, and the story still gets told.

ART CREATED BY KELLI NOTO

Supplies: *Cardstock; die-cut heart (Bazzill); patterned paper (AdornIt); die-cut letters and tabs (QuicKutz); clear labels (ChartPak); chipboard; ribbon; stamping ink*

Supplies: *Cardstock heart (Bazzill); patterned paper (Me & My Big Ideas); letter stickers (Making Memories, Me & My Big Ideas); rhinestones (Darice); heart stamp (Making Memories); acrylic paint; rickrack (Offray); envelopes (for pockets); pen*

Class Party

Paper doily hearts, construction paper boxes, pink cupcakes, and those cute store-bought valentines...we all have memories like these. To preserve the moment, creating a set of themed pockets is just the ticket to storing and displaying these treasured trinkets. Simply cut out the desired shape from cardstock and cut horizontal slits at random (or precise) intervals on the shape with a craft knife. Affix small envelopes to the back of the shape. Decorate the slit opening with ribbon, paper or trim. Adhere the assemblage to the background and slide in the ephemera.

ART CREATED BY ALECIA GRIMM

File It under "C" for Cute

Whether you choose a pre-made file folder album to decorate, or make one yourself out of tagboard, chipboard, cardstock or patterned paper, file folder albums are just plain cute! They are a perfect place to house pockets with slide-out journaling, pictures, tags, memorabilia or what-have-you. This type of album can be any theme, any color, or any size you choose! Use vellum to make translucent pockets that give you a peek at what lies within, or use patterned paper or cardstock to create opaque pockets you can decorate any way you like!

ART CREATED BY SUZY PLANTAMURA

Supplies: *File folder (Junkitz); cardstock; patterned paper, sticker accents (Daisy Bucket); rub-on letters and accents (7gypsies, Daisy D's); patterned transparency (My Mind's Eye); flowers (Heidi Swapp, Queen & Co.); brads; ribbon (Doodlebug, Making Memories, Maya Road); paper clips (AdornIt, Creative Imaginations); pen*

NICE WHEELS

ONE WAY

practically NEON

Photos: Sharon Winsler

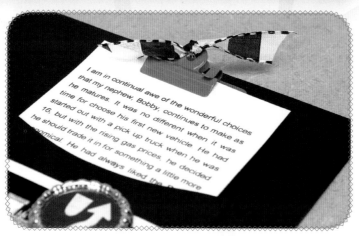

I am in continual awe of the wonderful choices that my nephew, Bobby, continues to make as he matures. It was no different when it was time for choose his first new vehicle. He had started out with a pick up truck when he was 16, but with the rising gas prices, he decided he should trade it in for something a little more ...omical. He had always liked the ...

Supplies: *Cardstock; die-cut letters (QuicKutz); journaling pocket (Bazzill); sticker accents (Design Originals, Karen Foster); brads; clipboard (Provo Craft); ribbon (Strano)*

Tease Them

Sometimes the best way to entice people to view our layouts is to tease them a little. By tucking a pocket so it is partially hidden behind the focal photo, and inserting the journaling so it's just peeking out of the top of the pocket, we create an eye-catching (yet subtle) way to tempt people to explore our layouts. Add a splash of bright color by attaching a unique "pull" for the journaling tab and your visual bait is complete!

ART CREATED BY LINDA HARRISON

Fun with Journaling

We all have them—those things in our life that eat (or devour) our time. This fun layout pays tribute to these distractions and showcases them with interactive journaling features. Lurking behind each flip-up photo block you'll find a tab to pull out hidden journaling, strips to slide out and a journaling block to swing open on a brad pivot. This interactive layout is a great way to use your leftover patterned paper and cardstock scraps. So get off the couch and create!

ART CREATED BY JODI AMIDEI

Supplies: *Cardstock; patterned paper (Colorbök, Frances Meyer, Paper Studio); brads; transparency; stamping ink; thread*

Apple Festival, September 16, 2006

carousel ride goes...

up

Always a hit, we can't pass up a carousel ride!

PULL

Up and Down on The Merry-Go-Round

Don't you just love carousels? Somehow they instantly whisk us back to childhood. It's fun to be a kid again riding a prancing steed as it gallops along. So why not recapture this timeless feeling on your layout? This clever slide feature could be used for so many themes and subjects. Use one to reveal hidden journaling or tuck another photo behind and watch it appear as you slide down the overlying photo. Think it's hard to do? Well, it's not! Don't worry, we'll walk you through step by step. Come play!

ART CREATED BY GRETA HAMMOND

You Gotta Try It!

1 Trim a strip of paper and adhere between the photo and mat.

2 Trim two slits onto the background paper large enough to fit the strip of paper through.

3 Slide the strip through the slits and back up to the front.

4 Using a glue dot, attach the circle chipboard embellishment to the end of the strip to act as a stop.

Tag-a-Long Photos

Tags are such a popular feature of scrapbooking layouts today. They are used for journaling, as mats for photos, and—in the case of this cheerful page—as a clever cover up for support photos. Attach decorated tags to the background using brads to create a pivot point for the tags. Hide photos underneath for a reverse on hidden journaling—here it's the photos that are hidden! The tags swing out of the way to reveal the little treasures underneath.

ART CREATED BY AMANDA WILLIAMS

Supplies: *Cardstock; metal charms, patterned paper, ribbon, tags (American Traditional); letter stickers (American Crafts, American Traditional, Making Memories); chipboard accents (American Traditional, Making Memories); brads (Making Memories); stamping ink; adhesive foam*

Record Time

Goals and achievements are fun and important things to chronicle in scrapbooks. But simply listing numbers, facts or other bits of data is really boring. Here's a fantastic way to really show how far a person has come, in whatever endeavor he or she is pursuing. With this changing element, when the tab is pulled, the information in the window changes right before your eyes. Refer to the steps for the "Making Magic Photos" project on page 56 for instructions on how to re-create this mechanism.

ART CREATED BY KELLI NOTO

Slide Show

There's nothing like a day at the beach. Take a sunny day at the ocean, add a couple of kids, and you have the makings for a layout with way too many photos to cram onto one page. Don't worry, you won't get buried up to your neck in the sand if you employ these ingenious slide-out panels to display the remaining support photos. Pull gently on the secondary photo on the layout...it's actually the visible end of a sliding photo panel! With this technique, it's possible to stow several pull-out panels on one layout!

ART CREATED BY NIC HOWARD

Supplies: *Cardstock; patterned paper (BasicGrey, Scenic Route); chipboard and rub-on letters (BasicGrey); letter stickers (BasicGrey, Provo Craft); rub-on accents (Memories Complete, Rhonna Designs, Scenic Route); corner rounder; stamping ink; thread; pen; Bookman Old Style font (Microsoft)*

Nature never ceases to amaze me. This wonder we found at Hot Water beach on the Coromandel peninsula is a perfect example. Hot Water Beach has hot springs which surface at low tide. They are not only hot, they are boiling! Mother Nature provides an incredible source of hot water, on a cold water beach. The day we were there, we dug our own little pool and it filled with hot thermal water, we soaked them in the pool right on the ocean's edge. Of course the beach is popular and the area of hot thermal springs is small, so you no sooner step out of your hot pool and someone steps in, but it is worth the hustle and bustle. We finished the visit to hot water beach off with a walk along the rocks. At which point Braden declared that I wasn't to take any more photos and took off running... Jan 2005.

The two of you are such a pair. Fighting one minute and snuggling the next. I can't figure it out myself, but I guess we can chalk it up to sibling rivalry. I hope someday you both will cherish your relationship. This fighting and being mean to each other is just a right of passage into adulthood. I pray that you will get past this phase and have a strong relationship one day. January 20..

Supplies: *Cardstock; patterned paper (Autumn Leaves, Hambly, My Mind's Eye); word accents (Creative Imaginations, My Mind's Eye); accordion mini album (Die Cuts With A View); flower accents (My Mind's Eye); buttons (Autumn Leaves, Buttons Galore); magnet (BasicGrey); transparency*

Accordion Lessons

Outside the scrapbooking world, the term "accordion" conjures up images of Lawrence Welk and his bubble machine. And the threat of accordion lessons sends shivers down kids' spines. But in here, it's a whole other concept altogether! Accordion albums have become a staple in scrapbooking. But how about incorporating one on a layout? Why not? It's a great way to add additional photos and journaling without using up precious layout space. A pair of opposing magnets help keep this accordion element from inadvertently opening up.

ART CREATED BY BECKY HEISLER

Treasure Chest

Creating interactive mini albums is a bit like burying a treasure chest. You fill it with wonderfully fun elements, vellum pockets to house slide-out journaling tags, flip-up panels, 3-D decorative elements that catch the eye and engage the viewer with bright colors, textures and shapes of all sizes and types. Then you sit back, and watch in delight as people discover the treasure trove you lay before them. Aye matey, thar dwells a pirate in all of us and 'tis easier than you think to turn a plain-Jane album into a treasure any inner-pirate would covet!

ART CREATED BY SUZY PLANTAMURA

Supplies: Cardstock; brads, patterned paper, sticker accents (Fancy Pants); patterned transparency (My Mind's Eye); chipboard letters, mini book, ribbon, ribbon slide, sheer flowers, velvet rickrack (Maya Road); rub-on accents (Fancy Pants, Maya Road); velvet paper (SEI); rhinestones (Me & My Big Ideas, unknown); chipboard shapes (Maya Road); glitter; mesh; clips (AdornIt, Provo Craft); staples; pen

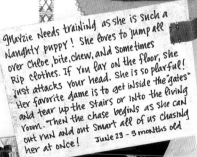

Mayzie Needs training as she is such a Naughty puppy! She loves to jump all over Chloe, bite, chew, and sometimes Rip clothes. If You lay on the floor, she just attacks Your head. She is so playful! Her favorite game is to get inside the "gates" and tear up the stairs or Into the living room. Then the chase begins as she can out run and out smart all of us chasing her at once! June 23 - 3 months old

I Now understand the term "Puppy Love." It is a feeling of

6.4

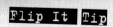

Think outside of the box with interactivity. Here are some cool ways to make your projects interactive with all the senses.

Include **swatches** of your favorite perfume in little plastic bags

Try **optical illusions** on your page

Add a **voice-recording** module

Add scent to your embossing powder with **unsweetened drink mix**

Add a pocket of **lollipops** to pull out

Make a **noise-maker** feature with paper engineering techniques

Use a small **music box** in an album

Include a **CD** of favorite music or additional photos

Put charms, macaroni, rice, beads and other small objects in a **shaker box**

Supplies: Foamcore; cardstock; patterned paper (BasicGrey); letters (Spellbinders); chipboard accents (Fancy Pants); wood skewer; flowers (Li'l Davis); handle (7gypsies); glitter glue; stamping ink; thread

Behind Closed Doors

It's just human nature to want to peek behind a closed door. So what better way to entice people to journey beyond the photos than to tuck the journaling or other narrative elements behind a door? Journaling is such an important feature of our scrapbooking, but let's face it, sometimes it detracts from the aesthetics of the layout. Discover how easy it is to incorporate doors in your layouts. Follow along as we guide you through the process. Go ahead, you don't even have to knock, the door's always open.

ART CREATED BY JEN LOWE

1 Using a craft knife or heat knife, trim an 8½" (22cm) square in the center of 12" x 12" (30cm x 30cm) foamcore, leaving a 1½" (4cm) margin on all sides. Push a wooden dowel rod into the foamcore along the top of the inside frame.

2 Cover the inside and outside edges with 2" x 12" (5cm x 30cm) strips of paper backed with adhesive. Cover the back of the frame with paper, pattern side up. Trim two 1" x 3" (3cm x 8cm) pieces of paper, fold over the dowel rod and tape together on the ends so they form tabs that move back and forth along the dowel rod.

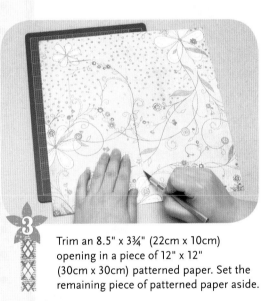

3 Trim an 8.5" x 3¾" (22cm x 10cm) opening in a piece of 12" x 12" (30cm x 30cm) patterned paper. Set the remaining piece of patterned paper aside.

4 Adhere tape to the top of tabs, then place the cut-out patterned paper on top of the tape.

5 Adhere the remaining piece of patterned paper to the top of the foamcore frame. Add a door handle to the piece of patterned paper that slides so it opens and closes easily.

It All STARTED INNOCENTLY ENOUGH

① ② ③ ④ ⑤

just a little lick of frosting...

¡PULL!

Supplies: Cardstock; scalloped cardstock (Bazzill); rub-on letters (Daisy D's, Hambly); decorative tape (7gypsies, Heidi Swapp); paper frill (Doodlebug); brads (Queen & Co.); solvent ink; pen; pop-up technique (Karen Burniston)

Pop-opᴇɴ Album

Lift-open albums have been done before. We've even shown you some. But this mini album has a whole new twist! When the tab is pulled, the album pops open before your eyes like magic! It's all thanks to the internal paper mechanics that lie beneath! This technique is the same concept as the "8 Years of Cakes" layout on the next page. It involves using a paper "beam" that attaches to a tab on the cover through a slit in the background. It's another example of how versatile this technique is!

ART CREATED BY SUZY PLANTAMURA

You'll Flip Over It

There is a paper engineer lurking in many of us just waiting for the opportunity to spread their mechanical wings. As we all know, hiding journaling under photos is a great way to preserve the artistic integrity of a layout's design. With this tab/flip mechanism, just pull the tab on the right of the page and all three photos magically flip up and over to reveal their journaling underneath. Each photo is adhered to an individual tab that feeds through a slit in the background and is affixed to a common paper "cross beam" on the back side of the layout. The end of this beam protrudes beyond the side of the layout and acts as the pull tab for this fun mechanism. See template on page 123.

ART CREATED BY KAREN BURNISTON

Supplies: *Cardstock; patterned paper (BasicGrey, KI Memories, Rusty Pickle); chipboard letters, letter stickers (Rusty Pickle); rub-on letters (Karen Foster); brads; clip (Making Memories); ribbon (Heidi Swapp, Mrs. Grossman's); sequins; Butterfinger, Quicky Script fonts (Internet downloads)*

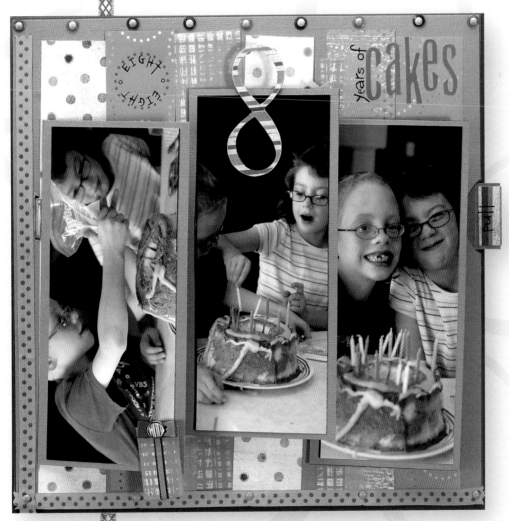

Supplies: Cardstock; patterned paper (Very Useful Paper Co.); lace (Wrights); adhesive foam; pen

Making Magic Photos

Looking at this layout is just like watching a magician pull a rabbit out of his hat. Tug on the tab and you'll "ooh and ahh" as the photo magically transforms from black-and-white to blazing full-blown eye-popping color in an effect that's sure to get your layout rave reviews. Magicians may not divulge their secrets, but we aren't magicians! Use the guidelines on the next page to construct the color-changing mechanism and you'll be making magic of your own in no time.

ART CREATED BY JODI AMIDEI

You Gotta Try It!

1 Print a horizontal 5" x 3½" (13cm x 9cm) photo twice: once in black-and-white and once in color. Trim each photo exactly in half. You should be left with four photo pieces measuring 2½" x 3½" (6cm x 9cm).

2 Adhere the left portion of the color print and right portion of the black-and-white print onto a strip of white cardstock. Crease the edges of the cardstock upward and set aside.

3 Trim a 10¾" x 3¾" (27cm x 10cm) strip of black cardstock. Use a craft knife to round the left edge. Adhere the right portion of the color photo to the black cardstock strip at the right edge. Trim a 2½" x 3½" (6cm x 9cm) window next to the color photo. Adhere the remaining left portion of the black-and-white photo on the other side of the window.

4 Slide the black cardstock strip under the creased edges of the white cardstock strip (be sure it can slide back-and-forth easily). Apply adhesive on the upper side of the creased edges to adhere to the backside of the layout background.

5 Trim a 4¼" x 3¼" (11cm x 8cm) window into a 12" x 12" (30cm x 30cm) piece of black cardstock. Adhere the white cardstock strip (with the black photo strip tucked in) behind the window so the black-and-white photo pieces meet.

OUT from behind

Linda

evidence

lift up

capture the moment photo art gallery proof

myself. I just thought it important to see the person behind all this photo-

Supplies: Cardstock; patterned paper (Li'l Davis); plastic letters (Heidi Swapp); die-cut letters and shapes (QuicKutz); letter stickers (Making Memories); button, flowers (Doodlebug); chipboard bookplate (BasicGrey); acrylic paint; stamp (Autumn Leaves); pigment ink; word stickers (7gypsies); floss; pen

Flower Power

Accordion books are a great way to add extra space for journaling. They are easy to create and very versatile, but let's face it...they've been "done" before. It's time to put the "petal" to the metal and let your layouts bloom. Simply take an accordion-folded piece of paper, adhere a magnet closure to it and top it with a bright and cheerful silk flower. Not only will you have that much needed extra space, you'll have a cheerful element for your layout and nobody will be the wiser that there's a book hidden underneath. You'll love it...you'll love it not...you'll love it...you'll love it not...YOU'LL LOVE IT!

ART CREATED BY LINDA HARRISON

Nice To Meet Ya

"Hello my name is..." This is the usual manner by which people introduce themselves—but scrapbookers, as we all know, are UNusual at best! This accordion-spined get-to-know-me album is a super fun way to include lots of information, whether it be juicy tidbits about the subject, or tons of hidden photos. And the size is totally up to you. All you have to do is glue mini envelopes crafted from patterned paper to the same side of each fold of an accordion spine. Add an additional row of envelopes to the opposite side of the folds for double accordion action. Slide in journaling cards or photos to finish. It's really a piece of cake.

ART CREATED BY SAMANTHA WALKER

Supplies: *Chipboard; cardstock; die-cut numbers, patterned paper, tab stickers (Creative Imaginations); letter stickers (American Crafts, Chatterbox, Creative Imaginations, Li'l Davis, Me & My Big Ideas); die-cut pockets (Sizzix); ribbon (Offray); corner rounder; Helvetica Medium Condensed font (Microsoft)*

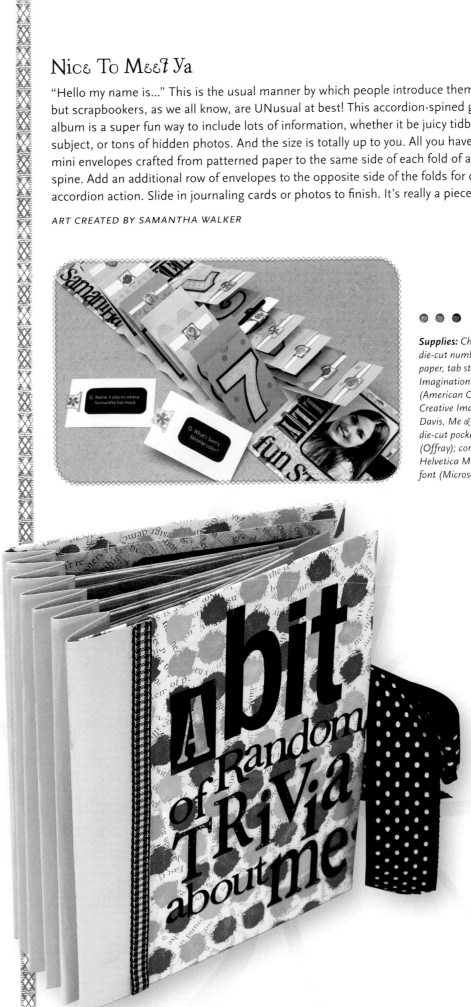

Supplies: Cardstock; patterned paper (BasicGrey); letter stickers (EK Success, Scenic Route); chipboard heart, number sticker (Making Memories); rub-on accent (Die Cuts With A View); buttons (Autumn Leaves); stamp (Hero Arts); stamping ink; pen

Slide into Fun

We know adding interactive elements to a layout is a new concept for many. But it doesn't have to be scary or intimidating. If you're just starting out on your adventure into interactiveness... start small! This fun little sliding feature is uber-easy. We're even here to hold your hand and guide you through the process! Little interactive features on a layout, like this sliding journaling block, can make a big difference in a layout's overall appeal. See template on page 120.

ART CREATED BY VICKI BOUTIN

1 Trim cardstock as shown. For the portion that will slide open, trim three sides and make two scores where the page will fold when opened. Make a small slit opening where the hidden element can slide through.

2 Adhere ¼" of the right edge of the horizontal strip to the back of the scored part of the slider. Slide the strip through the small slit.

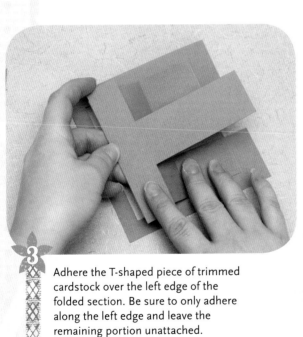

3 Adhere the T-shaped piece of trimmed cardstock over the left edge of the folded section. Be sure to only adhere along the left edge and leave the remaining portion unattached.

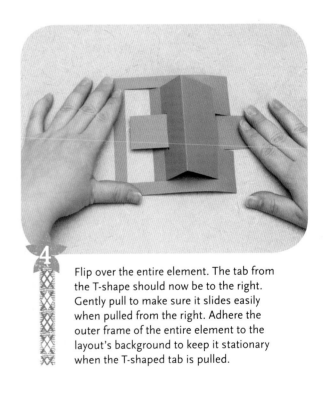

4 Flip over the entire element. The tab from the T-shape should now be to the right. Gently pull to make sure it slides easily when pulled from the right. Adhere the outer frame of the entire element to the layout's background to keep it stationary when the T-shaped tab is pulled.

Supplies: Cardstock; patterned paper (All My Memories, Creative Imaginations); film letters (Zsiage); chipboard shapes (Heidi Grace); stamps (B Line Designs); circle cutter; stamping ink

Dancing Ladies

There's nothing more intriguing than a layout that has moving elements. And this chic and sassy layout has a chorus line of moving elements, literally! Pull the tab and watch the ladies dance...all in different directions, all at the same time. Sound impossible? Hardly! This technique could be used for any subject or any theme. All it takes is a little paper engineering know-how. So go ahead, try your hand at being a paper engineer. You don't need a degree to make your pages dance. See template on page 120.

ART CREATED BY JEN LOWE

Free-Wheeling

One of the most important aspects of interactive scrapbooking is the "fun factor." This spinning, moving, roller-coaster feature will certainly put you on the right track! This technique is a more complex one that requires the crafter to brave the world of paper engineering. It may be more difficult to construct than other interactive features, but the results are worth it! As you pull the tab, the hidden journaling reveals itself, and the wheel spins as it moves along its track. There are many books available to teach the art of paper engineering techniques. Pick one up today and start playing!

ART CREATED BY KAREN BURNISTON

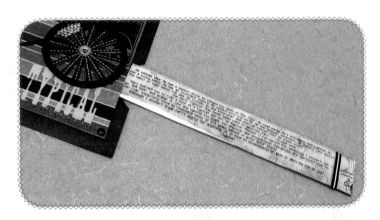

Supplies: *Cardstock; patterned paper (Paper Loft); chipboard brackets (Daisy D's); rub-on letters (Karen Foster, Rusty Pickle); rub-on stitching (My Mind's Eye); eyelets; brads (Making Memories); decorative tape (Heidi Swapp); rhinestones (Mark Richards); transparency; acrylic paint; cardboard; circle cutter; Sydnie font (Internet download)*

Flip It Tip

Looking for some food for thought? Check out this comprehensive list of books on paper engineering to help you experiment.

Cards that Pop-Up, Flip & Slide
by Michael Jacobs
(North Light Books, 2005)

The Elements of Pop-Up
by David A. Carter and
James Diaz (Little Simon, 1999)

Mathematical Origami
by David Mitchell (Tarquin, 1997)

Paper Automata
by Rob Ives (Tarquin, 1998)

Paper Engineering
by Natalie Avella
(Rotovision, 2003)

Paper Engineering for Pop-Up Books and Cards
by Mark Hiner (Tarquin, 1986)

Paper Pop Up
by Dorothy Wood
(David & Charles, 2007)

Pop Up! A Manual of Paper Mechanisms
by Duncan Birmingham
(Tarquin, 1999)

The Pop-Up Book
by Paul Jackson
(Owl Books, 1994)

Up-Pops
by Mark Hiner (Tarquin, 1993)

The Usborne Book of Paper Engineering
by Clive Gifford
(E.D.C. Publishing, 1997)

into the
bright

CHAPTER 3

The Skinny On Flipping & Spinning

Paper engineering. Such a technical and sterile sounding term for an otherwise fun and playful family of paper crafting techniques. It conjures up images of people in lab coats with pocket protectors and slide rules. It sounds so serious, but the only thing serious about interactive scrapbooking is that it is seriously FUN. From spinner pages to flip-up titles, journaling, photos or other flip-up elements, there is something in this chapter for anyone who wants to spice up a ho-hum layout. Take a spin around the creative dance floor with us with unique twists on traditional spinners. We guarantee you'll "flip" for these uber-fun interactive techniques. Think of this as Paper Engineering 101. It's a great place to start your adventures in interactivity!

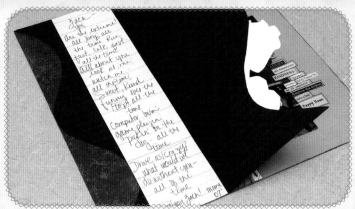

Supplies: Cardstock; patterned paper (BasicGrey, CherryArte, Creative Memories, Making Memories); chipboard letters (Heidi Swapp); sticker accents (Making Memories); buttons (Autumn Leaves, Buttons Galore); arrow stickers (EK Success); stamps (FontWerks); stamping ink; thread; pen

Hidden Panel

At first glance there is no hint that any part of this energetic layout is interactive. The page is dynamic as is, and the addition of journaling would detract from the overall energy flow this vibrant layout exudes. Becky cleverly camouflages her hidden journaling behind a panel right under the title that runs the entire length of her layout. By creating a full-length panel, the design is uninterrupted. This large lift-up panel also gives you plenty of extra space to tuck journaling or additional support photos.

ART CREATED BY BECKY HEISLER

Lucky Number

How do you get multiple photos on a page and not have it look overrun and chaotic? Hide them! Single-photo layouts are dramatic as all get out, but not very practical when you have a pile of photos staring at you, all begging to be included on your layout. Solution: enlarge the focal photo and turn it into a giant flap that opens up to conceal a page within a page. This technique gives you all the room you'll need to include every one of those precious memories!

ART CREATED BY KELLI NOTO

Supplies: *Cardstock; flower stamps, patterned paper (AdornIt); die-cut letters (QuicKutz); bleach; chalk ink*

Supplies: Cardstock; patterned paper (unknown); die-cut letters (QuicKutz); letter stickers (Making Memories); circle punch; brads; pen

Bowl Them Over

When you look at this page you can almost hear the pins crashing. The big, bold paper-pieced bowling pin embellishment is the perfect addition to this graphic layout. The bowling pin is just a simple, single-fold card that opens up to reveal the journaling inside. Just imagine the possibilities that exist for themes and schemes...they're literally endless. Think about all the "spare" room you'll gain on your layout with this technique!

ART CREATED BY LINDA HARRISON

Game On

Remember those childhood games with arrow spinners? How many times did we sit there and flick the arrow just for fun to watch it spin? It's super easy to bring that element into scrapbooking with this quick technique! Attach the pivot for the spinner (a circular foam spacer) to the background. Cut a circle that is slightly larger than the foam spacer from the middle of a decorated chipboard arrow. Place the arrow's hole over the foam spacer and cover the top of the foam spacer with a circle of cardstock that is slightly larger than the hole in the arrow. This construction allows for a free-spinning element that can be adapted to any shape or theme.

ART CREATED BY KELLI NOTO

Supplies: *Cardstock; die-cut letters (QuicKutz); chipboard; adhesive foam*

Supplies: Cardstock; patterned paper (Bam Pop); felt flowers, letter stickers (American Crafts); foam star (Darice); photo corners (Heidi Swapp); brads; pen

Pivot Point

It's so nice (and rare) when siblings actually get along. When those peaceful moments arise, we can't help but take massive amounts of photos of that blissfully calm moment. Then the question of what to do with all those photos comes next. One way to incorporate lots of photos and still include that oh-so-important journaling is to attach the photos to the background with a brad so each one pivots away to reveal the corresponding journaling underneath! The things kids say—they're priceless! So be sure to include them.

ART CREATED BY ALECIA GRIMM

Blowing in The Wind

There are some things that evoke immediate and spontaneous bursts of giggles. Pinwheels are one of these things. You can't help but smile when you see one. They're a happy part of childhood and they can help bring that feeling of glee to your layout. To aid in the spinning, separate the pinwheel from the background with a foam spacer. To create a pivot point, simply insert a straight pin through the center of the pinwheel, pierce through the foam spacers and then bend the pin to lay flat on the backside of the layout. Then all you have to do is blow!

ART CREATED BY CAROLINE IKEJI

Supplies: *Cardstock; patterned paper (American Crafts, Die Cuts With A View, KI Memories, Pink Martini, Scrapworks); letter stickers (American Crafts); chipboard letters, rhinestones (Heidi Swapp); pin (Heidi Grace); buttons; pen*

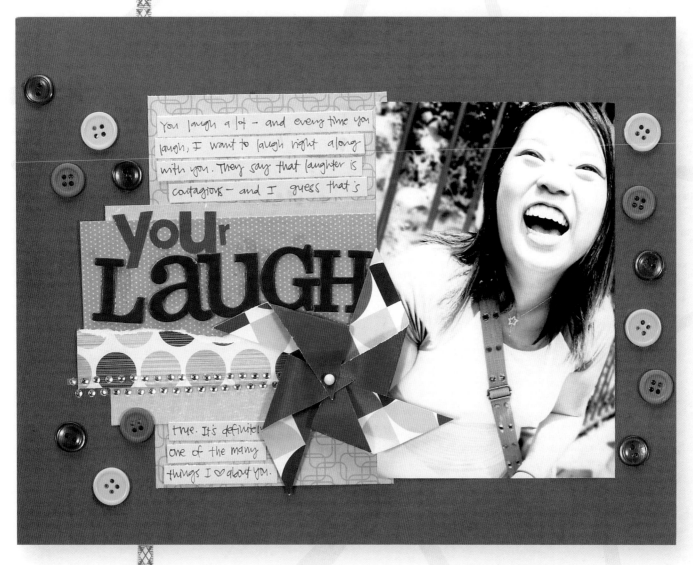

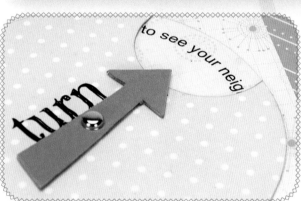

Supplies: *Cardstock; patterned paper, rub-on letters (Scenic Route); chipboard letters (Heidi Swapp); chipboard accents (Fancy Pants, Scenic Route); digital frame (Two Peas in a Bucket); brad; rub-on borders (Creative Imaginations); die-cut photo corner (QuicKutz); acrylic paint*

Turn of Phrase

Life is one big adventure...so why not incorporate a little of that adventurous spirit in your layouts? We all know how important journaling is to a layout. After all, it tells the story behind the pictures. But plain journaling blocks can be, well, tedious. Like digging for buried treasure in an archeological site, this journaling wheel encourages viewers to don their pith helmets and go exploring. Follow along and we'll guide you through this adventure in journaling step-by-step.

ART CREATED BY GRETA HAMMOND

1 Using word-processing software, print journaling in a circle format onto patterned paper. Trim into a circle using a craft knife or circle-cutting system.

2 Using a different piece of patterned paper, trim another circle of equal size to the first. Trim a small semicircle into the paper to serve as a window. Add an arrow, a rub-on word and any additional embellishments. Place the decorated circle over the full circle containing the journaling. Insert a brad through the arrow and both pieces of paper to allow the top circle to rotate over the bottom circle.

Letter from the Heart

Thanks to 12" x 12" (30cm x 30cm) formats for scrapbooking, it's easier than ever to include full-size sheets of journaling in your layouts without having to fold them. The entire front panel of this layout lifts up to reveal a hand-written letter in its heart. Score cardstock vertically about 1" (3cm) in from its edge. Secure the cardstock "flap" to the background with brads. Decorate the front of the "flap" as desired and add a tab for easy lifting. All that's left is to affix a heartfelt sentiment inside.

ART CREATED BY ALECIA GRIMM

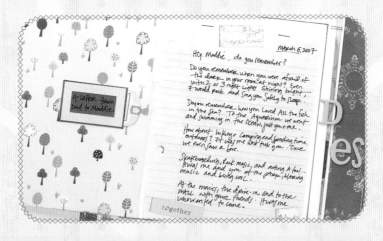

Supplies: *Cardstock; patterned paper, sticker accents (AdornIt); chipboard letters (Heidi Swapp); brads; staples; notebook paper; pen*

Supplies: *Cardstock; patterned paper (BasicGrey); chipboard letters (Heidi Swapp); rickrack; brads; pin (Heidi Grace); circle punch; corner rounder; adhesive foam; pen*

Document Closures

Putting flaps on a layout is a fabulous way to add either secret journaling or extra photos. Sometimes, however, these flaps just don't want to stay closed. It's easy-peasy to create closures for these flaps that are both decorative and completely functional as well. Punch circles of cardstock or patterned paper and affix them to the free edge of the flap with a brad. Affix a duplicate circle to the background with a brad. Wrap embroidery floss or string in a figure-eight pattern around the brads underneath the paper circle to keep your journaling safe and secure.

ART CREATED BY COURTNEY WALSH

Shake It Up

Most of us are familiar with shaker boxes. They are a playful way to add interest to a layout. But why stop there? There's no reason to limit this fun element to just a decorative detail. It's time to shake things up a bit, literally. Turn your entire layout into a shaker box. All you need is foamcore, a craft knife, some foam tape, a piece of acetate to cover it (hint: cut up a page protector or use a transparency), a little imagination and voilá! Think of it as creating a flat snow globe. How fun is that?

ART CREATED BY JODI AMIDEI

Supplies: *Cardstock; patterned paper (Very Useful Paper Co.); transparency (Grafix); stamps (PSX); ribbon (Michaels); solvent ink; crystal snowflakes (Jesse James Comp.); glitter flakes (Sulyn); adhesive foam; thread; pen*

The snowfall this year has been amazing — this storm started it all — it hit right before x-mas and even now we have snow on the ground that fell this December afternoon.

12/06

Winter in Colorado

CHILD HOOD

...may you always Remember these simple times...

Supplies: Cardstock; patterned paper, photo corners, tags (Heidi Grace); letter stickers (Doodlebug, Making Memories); chipboard letters, ribbon (unknown); pigment ink; buttons (Autumn Leaves); clip (Making Memories); magnetic clasp (BasicGrey)

Pockets, Pockets, Everywhere

Discovery is a big part of childhood; it's a trait that should be nurtured and fed on a regular basis. This accordion-style layout is the perfect way to do just that! Pull out the accordion feature of this page and delight in the joy of discovering the treasures hiding within each page's pocket. The pockets are a perfect place to house journaling and photos that chronicle the happiest of times—childhood itself. It's easy to adjust the number of pages in the accordion to suit your needs.

ART CREATED BY COURTNEY WALSH

What Lies Beneath

It is said that a picture is worth a thousand words, but who wants to be looking at that many words on a scrapbook layout? When you have a story to tell, you need room to tell it without having it dominate your layout altogether. Hurray for the hidden journaling flap! A larger focal photo or collection of photos arranged in one unit provide a terrific cover-up for extensive journaling. So now there is no excuse when it comes to including voluminous journaling... just hide it!

ART CREATED BY AMANDA WILLIAMS

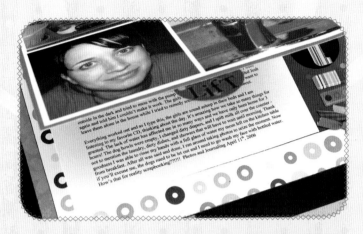

Supplies: *Cardstock; acrylic accents, die-cut letters, patterned paper (KI Memories); letter stickers (KI Memories, Me & My Big Ideas, Scrapworks); chipboard accents (Making Memories); circle punch; ribbon (Doodlebug, unknown); stamping ink*

Flip It Tip

Are you head over heels for flip elements? Here are some ideas to jazz up your flip features.

Use an empty flip-lid candy tin to house a mini-album

Make an inset door in foamcore

Turn your title into a flip-up feature

Cut out windows in the flip to give a glimpse of what lies within

Turn photos into flip elements

Use a mini file folder as a flip

Make a giant match book for a fun flip

in the heat of a summer day

there is nothing more enjoyed

than a MR whippy ice cream

while sitting on the front fence.

bliss

Cool Breeze · *play time* · *mr whippy* · *sun dresses* · *lazy days* · *melt* · *sunny* · *weather play* · *ice cream* · *quiet times* · *family* · *hot*

Supplies: *Cardstock; chipboard letters, patterned paper (Scenic Route); chipboard flower (Fancy Pants); rub-on letters (Heidi Swapp); rub-on accents (BasicGrey); tissue flowers (Prima); acrylic paint; brad; corner rounder; stamping ink; thread; pen*

Petal Pusher

He loves me, he loves me not, he loves me, he loves me not. No matter how the petals fall, we know you'll love this spinning flower accent! In addition to a fun element that whirls and twirls, the petals on the chipboard flower are large enough to include descriptive words that evoke a sense of time and place.

ART CREATED BY NIC HOWARD

1. Apply paint to a large chipboard flower and let dry. Add rub-on words. Be sure the words are facing the same direction on the chipboard flower so it is easy to read.

2. Find two chipboard circles to use as washers. Cover them with patterned paper if desired. Use a craft knife or a punch tool to create a hole through the middle of both pieces of chipboard.

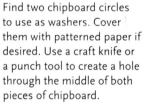

3. Assemble the spinning flower. The two washers lie directly on the layout, then the large chipboard flower, then a smaller paper washer and a brad. Note: It's possible to use only one chipboard washer but using two adds a bit of height so the flower spins easily.

EVERYDAY
MOMENTS

no matter how you turn, spin or twist it, life with you is always an adventure. You are one silly, sweet and sassy little girl!! The fun is in the EVERYDAY MOMENTS.

Supplies: *Cardstock; patterned paper (Making Memories, Scenic Route); chipboard accent (Scenic Route); letter stickers (Making Memories); brads; corner rounder; pen*

Peek-a-Boo

Sometimes we have more photos than we know what to do with—OK, most of the time. It's a continual struggle to incorporate lots of photos on a page without it looking chaotic and smushed. We have a solution for you! Just play peek-a-boo with your photos! By creating multiple layers of photos, one set hidden under the other, you can double, triple, or even quadruple the number of photos on your layout! Simply mat the top layers of photos on brightly colored paper and attach it with a brad to the background. Then it's a matter of swinging the top photo away to reveal more photos (or journaling if you like) underneath!

ART CREATED BY VICKI BOUTIN

Never Too Old

Board books are fun, but let's face it...board books can be, well, boring. It's time to come out from behind the shadows and play. Cover the pages of the book with decorative paper. Using large pre-made chipboard letters, adhere them to the right half of the face of each page. Carefully cut away the excess page underneath so each letter is silhouette cut along its outer edge. A spinning element adds zing to the cover of the book. Construct it using techniques that can be found in many paper engineering technique books (see page 63 for a list of good books to reference).

ART CREATED BY JEN LOWE

Supplies: *Cardstock; board book (C&T Publishing); letter structures (Zsiage); patterned paper (Paper Loft); rhinestones; stamps (Autumn Leaves, Plaid); stamping ink; paint*

SuNnErTime FuN!

SNY DaSSe JYd
SW Ming & spi ning
in GraN ad & Grandmas
Poo are The beSt
DaYs Of l

Photo: Deborah Ackerman

Flip It Tip

Is your head spinning? Here are some reasons spinning elements are so cool.

They are a great place to put tons of journaling

Perfect for serial action photos

A divine way to display chronological photos of someone as they age (school pics)

A fun way to feature thought bubbles for dialogues

Make silly face composites with changing features

Make a changeable wardrobe using patterned papers

Supplies: Cardstock; patterned paper (Die Cuts With A View); chipboard letters (Heidi Swapp); letter stickers (Making Memories); stamps (Sugarloaf); stamping ink; beads; decorative scissors; brad; pen

To Every Season, Turn, Turn, Turn

A book on interactive scrapbooking wouldn't be complete without a traditional "spinner" page. This tried-and-true technique has earned its place in the annals of scrapdom as a staple. Update the spinning feature by covering two chipboard circles with brightly colored papers and ransom-style journaling. The circle underneath is cut 1" (3cm) smaller than the top circle. Cut out a window in the top circle to reveal the changing photos and journaling underneath. Secure the circles with a brad and spin to your heart's content!

ART CREATED BY ALECIA GRIMM

File It Away

If you like the unencumbered look of a graphic-style layout but have too much to say and too many pictures, do we have a solution for you! Achieve this clean look by creating a file folder to house additional photos and journaling. There are many templates available out there you can use, or simply design your own. Adhere your focal photo on top of the file folder, attach it to the background and you're in business!

ART CREATED BY GRETA HAMMOND

Supplies: Cardstock; patterned paper, rub-on letters (Imagination Project); chipboard letters (Heidi Swapp, Imagination Project); letter stickers (Making Memories); brads; die-cut file folder (Provo Craft); photo turn (7gypsies); stamping ink

Supplies: *Cardstock; patterned paper (B Line, Crafty Secrets, Design Originals, Scrapperdashery); charms (Two Purple Pandas); stamps (After Midnight, Jen Lowe Designs, My Sentiments Exactly); clips (Design Originals); stamping ink*

Child at Heart

We may grow older, but growing up is totally optional. There is a kid inside us all who, despite the stacking years, is longing for adventure and never forgets to laugh! Here is a fun mini-book, chock full of cut-out windows and flip-down flaps just begging to be decorated and filled with humorous photos and quips of years gone by. Silhouette cut hand-tinted black-and-white photos for an extra level of playfulness. Add journaling strips using a vintage typewriter font for added effect. Let loose and decorate your mini-book with total abandon!

ART CREATED BY JEN LOWE

Title Peek-a-Boo

Glimpses...this page is all about glimpses. It is designed to make you want to peek inside to see what's lurking behind the title. Create a cardstock flap and stamp and heat emboss letters onto the outside of the flap to spell the title. Using a craft knife, cut out the centers of the letters to create windows in the flap. Adhere a transparency strip to the back of the flap to further the window effect. Attach a top flap to the background of the layout and tuck photos behind the flap.

ART CREATED BY SUZY PLANTAMURA

Supplies: *Cardstock; patterned paper (Crossed Paths, Daisy D's); epoxy letter (Karen Foster); chipboard hearts (Heidi Swapp); photo turns (7gypsies, Queen & Co.); brads (Queen & Co.); acrylic paint; embossing powder; floss; solvent ink; stamps, transparency (unknown); pen*

Photos: Jamie Harper Photography

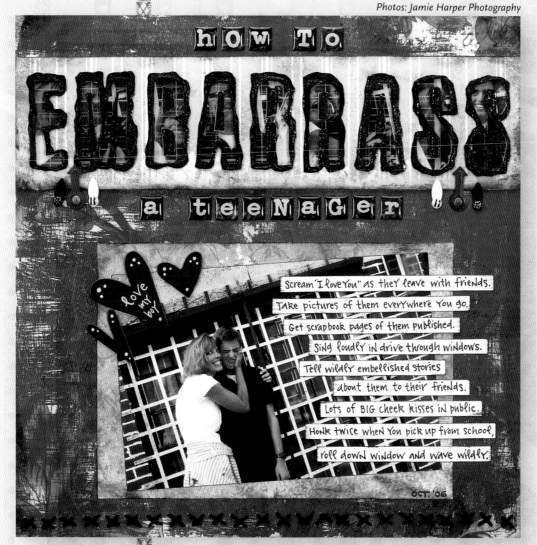

how to EMBARRASS a teeNaGer

Scream "I love You" as they leave with friends.
Take pictures of them everywhere You go.
Get scrapbook pages of them published.
Sing loudly in drive through windows.
Tell wildly embellished stories
about them to their friends.
Lots of BIG cheek kisses in public.
Honk twice when You pick up from school,
roll down window and wave wildly.

OCT. '06

Easy Breezy

Dandelions, ladybugs, children's smiles and pinwheels...it's the little things in life (most often overlooked) that bring us great joy. This pinwheel feature is easy to create and adds a whimsical element that's not only beautiful to look at, but fun to play with! You can either use double-sided paper to create the pinwheel, or use two pieces of paper adhered to each other back to back. For the pinwheel's handle, a decorative paper- covered straw is just the ticket you'll need to complete this fun element. See template on page 122.

ART CREATED BY BECKY HEISLER

Supplies: *Cardstock; patterned paper (BasicGrey, K&Co.); rub-on letters and accents (BasicGrey); round transparency (Chatterbox); buttons (Autumn Leaves, Buttons Galore, Die Cuts With A View); embossing powder; brad; ribbon; thread; pen*

Print or sketch a pinwheel pattern and lay it over cardstock. Lightly adhere the corners down with temporary adhesive. Trim along the solid lines; decorate both sides and add journaling. Punch holes in each of the four corners and the center. Trim along the dotted lines from the four corners to the center circle. Stay approximately 1½" (4cm) from the center.

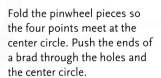

Fold the pinwheel pieces so the four points meet at the center circle. Push the ends of a brad through the holes and the center circle.

Use a tack or sharp point to poke a hole through the top of a straw. Carefully push the sharp point through the straw at about ½" (13mm) from the top. Place the straw on the backside of the pinwheel and push the ends of the brad through the hole in the straw. Flatten the brad on the backside of the pinwheel to secure everything together.

Supplies: *Cardstock; patterned paper (Karen Foster); patterned transparency (Hambly); chipboard letters (Li'l Davis); acrylic paint; ribbon (Doodlebug); brad; pen*

Ready, Set, Action

Serial action shots can be lackluster on their own, but when you arrange them behind a spinner, something magical happens! The photos come alive with motion! Create a traditional spinner with a quarter window out of cardstock and crop photos in one-quarter pie pieces. Attach photos to the background and affix the spinner over the photos with a brad. Add die-cut or chipboard letters around the spinner for a fun title. Journaling around the outside edge of the spinner furthers the sense of movement on this dynamic layout.

ART CREATED BY SUZY PLANTAMURA

Come To Your Senses

It's time for creating an interactive page that goes beyond adding kinetic features to touch and see. What about incorporating elements that evoke responses from your other senses? Hide zippered bags containing perfume-saturated pieces of cotton in alcoves that are recessed into foamcore (behind little cardstock flip-up doors). Include journaling with descriptive details about each scent. It is said that olfactory memories are the strongest. So why not include some in your layouts and memory art projects? This is a great way to take scrapbooking to the next sensory level!

ART CREATED BY JODI AMIDEI

Supplies: *Cardstock; patterned paper (7gypsies, K&Co.); stamps (Hero Arts, Plaid); enclosures (Colorbok); ribbon (Hobby Lobby); foamcore; gold leaf pen (Krylon)*

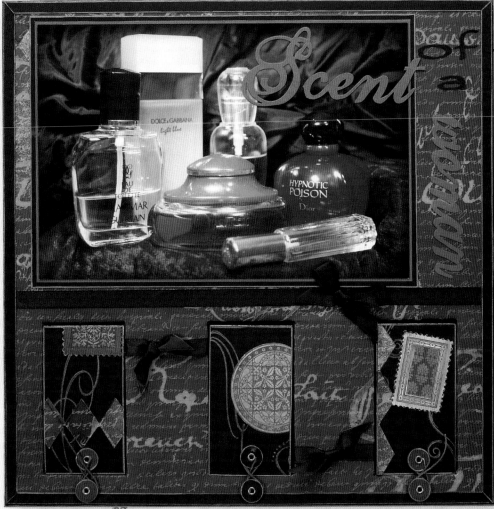

Photo: Torrey Scott

Supplies: *Cardstock; patterned paper (Dream Street, SEI); letter stickers (Chatterbox, Creative Imaginations, Making Memories); epoxy stickers, rickrack (SEI); thread; image editing software (Adobe)*

Dial a Month

The first year of life is chock-full of milestones. Every month heralds new and exciting skills that deserve to be documented in their entirety. This spinner page does just that. It allows the reader to "dial a month" and read about the accomplishments in detail. But you're not limited to recording only the first year of life; this spinning technique can chronicle any major event or milestone. School years, the months of pregnancy, personal accomplishments or goals, or even a recurring event such as an annual family reunion or holiday celebration are all worthy of documentation through pictures and journaling.

ART CREATED BY SAMANTHA WALKER

1 Create a circle using image-editing software. Insert a rounded-corner box that will serve as a window and a small, cropped photo above the box. Print the entire circle onto photo paper. Using a craft knife, trim the circle and around the small rounded-corner box to create the window.

2 Adhere onto chipboard or cardboard for durability (remember to trim around the window in the cardstock as well) and decorate with die-cut letters or as desired. Set aside.

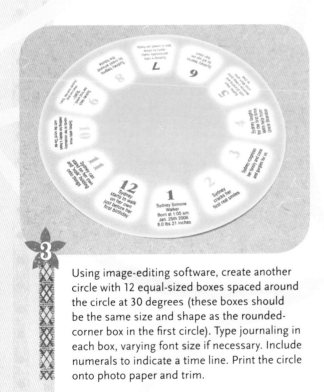

3 Using image-editing software, create another circle with 12 equal-sized boxes spaced around the circle at 30 degrees (these boxes should be the same size and shape as the rounded-corner box in the first circle). Type journaling in each box, varying font size if necessary. Include numerals to indicate a time line. Print the circle onto photo paper and trim.

4 Use a brad to adhere the chipboard-mounted circle above the circle containing the journaling. The brad will secure the two circles together and will allow the top circle to rotate over the bottom. Secure the bottom circle to your layout background using adhesive.

On looking back through my layouts during the past year or so, there are a lot about Abby and her two-year old behaviour. I have enjoyed being able to see the humorous side in what is a tough time; the terrible twos are never easy for any parent. Through it, of course, we loved our little girl to pieces and knew she was just finding her footing, learning how to find independence in this world.

Abby is now three years old and I was just thinking how she has changed recently. All of a sudden she and I are friends again. She is a confident, assertive young girl, but she is sensible and the tantrums are disappearing. I really feel like we have been through a tunnel and now we are coming out

Supplies: *Cardstock; patterned paper (Crafter's Workshop, Rouge de Garance, Scenic Route); rub-on letters and accents (American Crafts, Rouge de Garance); solvent ink; chipboard flower (Maya Road); corner rounder; pen*

Half Moons

There are milestones in life, and making it through the "terrible twos" is definitely one that calls for major celebrations (and maybe a tranquilizer or two). This fun take on a traditional spinner page employs a spinner that is only a half of a whole. A series of chipboard washers and a brad provide the foundation for the spinning element. While the photo remains stationary, the green half spins around to expose the red half and uncover the singular sentiment of the page...that beyond the darkness there is, indeed, a light at the end of the toddler tunnel. See template on page 124.

ART CREATED BY NIC HOWARD

Flap, Flap, Flap

It's all about the details when it comes to documenting a wedding day: the kiss, the flowers, the hair. With this flap technique, your photos are doubled, instantly. Each photo on the page is a flap, under which lies another photo of the same size and shape. The journaling hides beneath the photos as well and is a welcomed surprise when the flaps are lifted up. With this technique it is possible to maintain an overall sense of elegance and balance by reserving white space while still incorporating loads of photos and information.

ART CREATED BY SAMANTHA WALKER

Supplies: *Cardstock; ribbon (BasicGrey); brads; metal corners (Making Memories); Floralia, P22 Cezanne fonts (Internet download)*

She changes clothes sometimes 20 times a day. Her look has to be just right. If it's not, she goes through outfit after outfit until she comes up with the perfect ensemble. She primps in front of the mirror for what seems like an eternity. Haley, she's a closet diva.

Wheel-O-Fashion

Playing dress-up is part of growing up! We have all been closet divas at some point in our lives. It's only "fitting" that we carry it onto our scrapbook layouts. Now, changing clothes is easy! Just turn the wheel on the spinning element and watch her outfits change. All you need to get started is a large photo with simple clothing to create the framework for this unique spinning dress-up feature. Use the following steps to re-create this stylish spinning feature. It's time to take our love of fashion to the next level!

ART CREATED BY TORREY SCOTT

● ● ●

Supplies: *Cardstock; patterned paper (Hot Off The Press, MOD, My Mind's Eye); chipboard; ribbon (Chatterbox, KI Memories); brad; transparency; chalk ink; lacquer topcoat (Plaid); adhesive foam*

1 Print a photo and trim a hole over the element you'd like to change pattern (in this example it is the photo subject's shirt). Position the photo over your patterned paper or cardstock background and trim a corresponding hole in the paper.

2 Trim a circle out of chipboard or cardboard. Using a protractor, divide the circle into equally sized segments. Trim coordinating patterned papers to fit over each segment. Cover the inside borders (or seams) of the patterned paper with ribbon or rickrack for added interest.

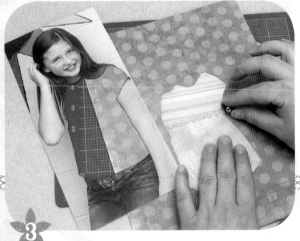

3 Secure the circle under the photo using a hidden brad as a pivot point. Be sure to allow a portion of the circle to stick out from underneath to let viewers spin the circle. Add additional stationary circles or half circles to playfully stick out from other sides if desired. Add a "turn" label to the circle that spins.

Flip It Tip

Think outside of the box by taking interactivity out of the album and on to other projects.

Just the thing for creating hands-on art for the wall

Wow them with interactive jewelry

Perfect for making mini albums

Great for making cards

Wonderful for work presentations or school projects

Fabulous for making fun rainy-day activities

A Passion for Pop-Ups

When we think of interactive scrapbooking, pop-ups are one of the first things

that, well, pop up in our minds. After all, who didn't love pop-up books as a kid? And for

many of us, pop-up elements are synonymous with interactivity because of our love of these

interactive books in childhood. To re-create pop-up features may look a little intimidating

at first glance, but once you get the basics of how the underlying mechanisms of pop-

up features work, the sky is the limit. We offer an array of techniques for all skill

levels. It's so easy to adapt pop-up elements to any theme, scheme, scale

or shape. Whether you're a beginner or seasoned scrapbooker,

before long you'll be the queen of 3-D and the life of

every scrapbooking party.

Are you a fold fanatic? Do you know the difference between a mountain fold and a valley fold? Fear not! We've got it all spelled out for you.

Mountain Fold
To create a mountain fold, fold the paper away from you and crease along the dashed or dotted line. You should be left with a crease that resembles a mountain peak.

Valley Fold
To create a valley fold, fold the paper towards you and crease along the dashed or dotted line. You should be left with a crease that resembles a valley.

Supplies: *Cardstock; scalloped cardstock (Bazzill); chipboard circle, patterned paper (Scenic Route); chipboard letters (Heidi Swapp); rub-on accent (Chatterbox); buttons (Wal-Mart); floss; ribbon (unknown); pen*

Spring into Action

What happens when you mix hidden journaling, a big lift up flap, and a fun pop-up element? You get a great layout, that's what! There are many ways to create the foundation mechanism behind a pop-up feature. To create one like Courtney's, fold a large piece of cardstock in half. Trim a photo and large patterned paper arrow (or any other shape you desire) and score down the middle. Adhere the photo and arrow along the crease of the cardstock flap by placing these elements on an accordion-folded strip of paper so the elements "pop" when opened. You've just created a paper spring that will lift your elements off the page! How easy was that?

ART CREATED BY COURTNEY WALSH

A Fish Story

There is something quite fishy about this layout. Somehow you get the feeling there is something lurking just under the surface...AH HA! Lift up the title flap and a school of pop-up fish greet you! The base for this fishy pop up is made by cutting pairs of parallel vertical slits in the background of the fold-out card and mountain-folding each resulting strip at a 90 degree angle. Mount whatever shapes you desire atop each strip on the vertical surface to create a whimsical 3-D scene. Reference page 104 for a similar technique.

ART CREATED BY KELLI NOTO

Supplies: *Cardstock; patterned paper (Creative Imaginations); wood veneer (unknown); die-cut letters and tab (QuicKutz); letter stamps (Technique Tuesday); clear adhesive label (ChartPak); chalk ink; adhesive foam*

Catching fish had never been so important. Midway through their ten-day trip, John and Eric hit a patch of rapids that overturned their canoe. Much of their food was lost. Some of what they did salvage was sodden with river water and soon spoiled. They were in the middle of Canada's Boundary Waters where you can go weeks without seeing another person so swinging by the grocery store for more provisions was out of the question. If they wanted to eat, they had to catch their own dinner. They have always practiced catch-and-release fishing, but this time they had to catch to survive.

I am loving your latest phase. You are cuddly, affectionate and down right adorable. My days are filled with hugs and kisses and sweet words. You hold my face in your hands, making sure I am paying attention, and then you whisper sweet nothings to me, expressing what is in your heart. Pure, sweet innocence flowing from your lips and pure joy for me. I hope this phase never ends.

tell me what is in YOUR heart

sWeet

NOtHiNGs

Supplies: *Cardstock; patterned paper (Creative Imaginations, Fancy Pants); chipboard letters and shape, ribbon (Fancy Pants); letter stickers (EK Success); rub-on words (Creative Imaginations); die-cut hearts (Provo Craft); key hole (Melissa Frances); digital frame (Two Peas in a Bucket); hinges (Making Memories); acrylic paint*

From The Mouths of Babes

Kids say the darndest things: phrases that make us giggle, make us groan, some even make us wonder if these children are really related to us. Kid-isms, quotes, poetry, descriptors—so many treasured bits of wisdom abound. They deserve a special place of honor in our scrapbooking. Hidden behind this decorated chipboard heart lay tiny individual pop-up paper shapes with priceless quips written on them. Whether you pop them off the page with foam spacers, or use accordion-folded paper supports as shown here, these mini pop-ups are a breeze to make.

ART CREATED BY GRETA HAMMOND

From The Heart

Hidden pop-up elements are a fun and funky way to jazz up hidden journaling. They provide an unexpected bit of "wow" factor when the journaling is revealed. For an extra kick, try journaling onto a simple shape (like this heart). Mountain-fold the shaped journaling block down the middle; add valley-fold tabs or smaller shapes as feet to secure it to the inside face of the folder. To ensure proper alignment when adhering it to the folder, cover the tabs with adhesive and secure the shape first to one side of the folder, then collapse the shape and cover with the other side of the folder. Now, when the folder is opened, the journaling shape will pop up and say, "Hello!"

ART CREATED BY CAROLINE IKEJI

Supplies: *Cardstock; patterned paper (American Crafts, KI Memories, Li'l Davis); letter stickers (American Crafts); rub-on accents, tab sticker (KI Memories); decorative tape (Heidi Swapp); acrylic paint; pen*

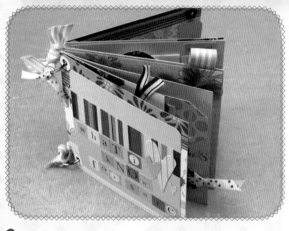

Supplies: *Cardstock; heart accents, letter and word stickers, patterned paper, rub-on accents (Heidi Grace); buttons (Autumn Leaves); envelopes (Making Memories); brads (Chatterbox); ribbon (Chatterbox, Offray); book rings; floss; pen*

Lesson in Dissection

When we think of dissection, the first thing that comes to mind is unfortunate little frogs in biology class. Thank goodness this is scrapbooking and not biology! The inspiration and how-tos for this mini-book came from dissecting a children's pop-up book, not a frog. Hey, disassembling a pop-up book is a great way to learn how pop-up mechanisms work. But you don't have to do that for this project! We'll supply you with the steps it takes to re-create the pop-up features in this fun, versatile mini-album. Disclaimer: No frogs were harmed in the making of this pop-up album, although it is "ribbet"-ing.

ART CREATED BY COURTNEY WALSH

You Gotta Try It!

1 Using a craft knife or punch, trim a heart or other shape from patterned paper. Fold heart exactly in half.

2 Trim a small strip of cardstock and fold accordion-style into six sections.

3 Adhere the middle section of strip to the back of the heart along the crease. Be sure the adhesive is only applied to the two middle sections.

4 Attach the entire piece over two album pages by laying the crease of the heart along the gutter. Apply adhesive to the two outer sections of the cardstock strip to securely glue it to the album pages.

Spread Your Wings

Sshhh. Perhaps if you're quiet, this lovely butterfly will come to light gently on your hand. What do you mean, "it's not real"? OK, so it's a fanciful pop-up feature...but it does breathe life into this soothing layout. You, too, can create beautiful little pop-up elements like this for your pages. Turn to the Internet or a paper engineering book (see list on page 63) for templates and inspirational ideas. Then pull out a craft knife and your favorite patterned paper to trim fanciful shapes that pop when opened. You'll be pleasantly surprised at what appears before your eyes.

ART CREATED BY NIC HOWARD

Supplies: *Cardstock; patterned paper (BasicGrey); chipboard letters (CherryArte, Heidi Swapp); letter stickers (American Crafts); solvent ink; beads; thread; glass finish topcoat (Plaid); pen*

Photos: Jacob Howard

Supplies: Cardstock; patterned paper (SEI); chipboard word and accents (Fancy Pants); acrylic paint

What's In a Name?

When we think of pop ups, the image that usually comes to mind is a scored and bent "platform" on which to adhere an embellishment or photo. But pop ups can be so much more. It's really quite simple to create a strikingly subtle 3-D pop-up title using only your craft knife and some cardstock. Honest. What a great way to personalize a layout or card. And the sweet thing is, this technique will work with any name or word. The following steps will lead you through the process. You'll be amazed at how easy this stunning technique truly is.

ART CREATED BY LINDA HARRISON

You Gotta Try It!

1 Arrange the title word in block type using word-processing software. Add journaling under the title word. Print onto cardstock and trim to the desired size.

2 Fold in half across the title.

3 Using a craft knife, trim the vertical lines of the title.

4 Fold the letters out toward you while folding the cardstock in half. The title letters should pop up from the page.

Make Your Photos Pop

Travel photos from exotic places deserve special treatment—something dramatic to make them really pop. The base for this layout is actually a giant card that opens to reveal the splendor inside. Each focal photo is matted on cardstock with 1" (3cm) tabs on each side that are adhered underneath blocks of cardstock on the layout's background. A strip of transparency, fed through a slit in the photo and hidden underneath, acts as the mechanism that pulls the photos into an arch as the card is opened. To create an eye-catching title, affix die-cut or sticker letters to a strip of transparency and adhere to the back of the photos.

ART CREATED BY KAREN BURNISTON

Supplies: *Cardstock; letter stickers, patterned paper, tags (BasicGrey); chipboard letters (Cloud 9); labels (Around the Block); arrow tab (7gypsies); brads; clip tabs (Making Memories); eyelets; art tape (Times to Cherish); flower (Prima); transparency; Franklin Gothic Medium Condensed font (Internet download)*

Supplies: *Board book (Judy's Stone House); cardstock; patterned paper (My Mind's Eye, Shalom Scrapper); rub-on accents (My Mind's Eye); stamps (Autumn Leaves, Crafty Secrets, Stampers Anonymous); letter stamps (Plaid); embossing powder; charms (Two Purple Pandas); die-cut shapes (Spellbinders); stamping ink; glitter glue; brads, photo turns (Creative Impressions); ribbon (American Crafts, Darice, Offray)*

Light a Candle

This book has such a feeling of old-world charm. Distressing inks and rich, warm colors give it an ancient appearance...as though it were some treasure waiting to be unearthed as it lies buried in the sands of time. And what treasures lie within it! Among the beautiful photos and heartfelt journaling are scattered little pop-up features. Come on! Don't be afraid...it's time to explore! See templates on page 124.

ART CREATED BY JEN LOWE

Piece of Cake

Always wanted to include a fun little pop-up element on your layout, but didn't know how? Close your eyes, make a wish, and blow out the candles. WOW. Your wish just came true! Just lift up the little card and voilá! It's like opening a birthday present. And, there's a surprise too! You can use any theme, any shape to form the pop-up feature. Just cut out your desired shape (plus a little extra on both sides for tabs) from cardstock, fold it in half, fold in the little tabs on both sides and adhere it to the inside of a mini-card. It's your birthday! It's your birthday!

ART CREATED BY LINDA HARRISON

Supplies: *Cardstock; transparent letter (Heidi Swapp); die-cut letters (QuickKutz); rub-on cake (BasicGrey); dimensional and letter stickers (unknown); round sticker (Memories Complete); brads; floss*

Supplies: Cardstock; chipboard flower, patterned paper (Imagination Project); acrylic title (Jo-Ann's); rub-on letters and accents (Imagination Project, Scrapworks); shaker bubble (Pebbles); journaling tag (7gypsies); brads; photo turns; pen

It's What's Inside That Counts

Just like Clark Kent, this page has an unassuming exterior. It's so easy to take a "plain Jane" page and give it some "wow" by simply adding a hidden pop-up feature. Just lift the main photo to reveal its playful interior. Simply fold a piece of cardstock in half and fold inward along a pair of opposing diagonal scores in the middle at the top. Then cut two parallel slits across the middle near the bottom and fold the piece inward to create the platforms on which to mount photos, journaling or embellishments. See template on page 121.

ART CREATED BY VICKI BOUTIN

Hope Springs Eternal

Know someone who is feeling down-in-the-dumps? This bright and sunny mini-album would be the perfect gift to lift their spirits. Pop-up elements abound throughout this beautiful tribute to friendship. The foundation for many of the pop-up features in this book all stems from the same base pattern—a mountain-folded cardstock triangle with tabs on both sides to secure it to its background. From there, all it takes is a little imagination and some fun cut-out shapes or silk flowers to turn this versatile pop-up feature into anything you want!

ART CREATED BY JEN LOWE

Supplies: *Mini album (Die Cuts With A View); cardstock; patterned paper (BasicGrey); ribbon, tags (7gypsies); eyelets (Eyelet Outlet); brads (Making Memories); clips, sticker accents (Bo-Bunny); transparency; crystals (Creative Crystal Co.); stamps (After Midnight, Endless Gizy, Hero Arts, Penny Black, Plaid, Wordsworth); stamping ink*

Inspiration can be found all around us. Don't pass over these sources of creativity when creating interactive layouts.

Children's pop-up books
Museums (especially children's museums and art museums)
Board games
Toys
Origami
Garage sales
Flea markets
Internet

Flip It Tip

In The Fold

Looking for that last-minute gift? Or perhaps, you want to send more than "just a card" to family and friends? Look no further! This beautiful accordion album may look complex and detailed, but it's really easy-peasy to re-create...even with its pop-up Christmas tree feature! HONEST! We'll help you out with some instructions to assemble this interactive album. Pop-up elements are a piece of cake once you learn the basics. All it takes is a little know-how!

ART CREATED BY KELLI NOTO

You Gotta Try It!

1 Fold the cardstock and draw a tree pattern.

2 Carefully trim the solid lines, leaving the dotted lines intact.

3 Score the dotted lines and carefully fold back in both directions.

4 Open the paper like a tent and poke each section through to the other side.

Music Box Dancer

Most of us remember and treasure childhood jewelry boxes that have a little ballerina that pops up and twirls to the music when you open the lid. Here is a great way to bring that memory to life in the form of a mini-album. In this example, Torrey trimmed two pieces of heavy cardstock into the shape of an umbrella with tabs on each end to glue them together. But before adhering them, she tied rubber bands on each end to provide the tension that causes the from to spring open when its cover is released. How perfect would this album be to showcase that special little dancer in your life?

ART CREATED BY TORREY SCOTT

● ● ●

Supplies: *Frame box (Plaid); cardstock; patterned paper (Cosmo Cricket); glitter; acrylic paint; chalk ink; trim (May Arts, Wrights); ribbon (Hobby Lobby); clear lacquer (Sakura); corner punch; costume jewelry (Wal-Mart, Wilton); rubber band*

Megan has been dancing since she was a tiny little girl. She is so graceful, and her movements are fluid as she glides across the stage. Seeing her in this soft pink tutu reminded me of those music boxes we all had as girls...the kind when you open up the lid, the little ballerina pops us and starts to pirouette to the music. ....Dance, ballerina, dance...

Photos: Beth Huter

Flip It Tip

Need some paper engineering 101? Here are a few tips to get you started.

Buy a children's pop-up book and carefully disassemble it to see how it works.

Work in a well-lit area.

Make certain your measurements and cutting are precise and accurate.

Read all instructions before you begin.

Start with simple techniques.

Use a bone folder or back of a spoon to flatten creases.

Make and save examples and templates of your projects.

Invest in a good paper engineering technique book (see page 118).

Be brave! Give paper engineering a try and you'll soon see how fun and addictive it really can be!

Supplies: *Foamcore; cardstock; patterned paper (My Mind's Eye); ribbon (Chatterbox, Michaels, Offray); rickrack (Wrights); brads; transparency; chipboard;* Slinky™ *toy; stamping ink*

Put Some Spring in Your Step

Traditional pop-up elements are usually created using paper engineering techniques...but they don't have to be. Any spring will do! For small elements, the springs inside ballpoint pens work well, and for full-page scale pop-up features like this, a Slinky™ is the perfect addition to help your photos "spring" to life. It's easy to construct this kicky page using a foamcore base with inset door to house the layout inside. To attach the Slinky™, simply poke a hole in the foamcore and feed it into the inner core. To secure on back, insert its end through the chipboard backing and secure with tacky tape on the back side.

ART CREATED BY JODI AMIDEI

Fun Surprise

Just like an Easter egg hunt, this layout has fun hiding in unexpected places! Push the photo turn away, lift up the photo and voilá! Fun pops out at you...literally. This type of pop up is the easiest to create. It uses a "U"-shaped cardstock platform with folded tabs on both ends to create the lifted feature. Adhere the one tab to the inside of the cover and the other tab to the background. Decorate the front of the platform with words, photos or other embellishments and you're good to go! See template on page 122.

ART CREATED BY ALECIA GRIMM

Supplies: *Patterned paper, rub-on accents (Fancy Pants); chipboard letters (Autumn Leaves); photo turn; brad; stamping ink; pen*

Supplies: *Cardstock; patterned paper (K&Co., Making Memories, Paper Adventures); brads, letter stickers, rickrack (Making Memories); acrylic paint; velvet rickrack (BasicGrey, Maya Road); chipboard flowers (Maya Road); fabric (unknown); glitter; rhinestones (Paper Adventures); chalk ink; paper trim (Doodlebug); felt; fibers (BasicGrey, unknown); transparency; watercolors; adhesive foam*

Play Time

Interactive pages are meant to be touched, but this one goes beyond that. This fanciful layout invites you not only to touch and feel it, but also to stay and play with it! Your kids, and yes even you, will love to play dollhouse again. It's a fun and unique layout that truly invites the viewer to participate on a whole new level. Step by step, we'll lead you through re-creating this playful layout. Come on! It's play time.

ART CREATED BY SUZY PLANTAMURA

1 Using a pencil, lightly draw a house on a piece of 12" x 12" (30cm x 30cm) white cardstock.

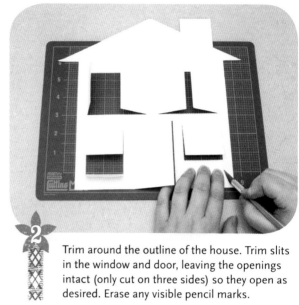

2 Trim around the outline of the house. Trim slits in the window and door, leaving the openings intact (only cut on three sides) so they open as desired. Erase any visible pencil marks.

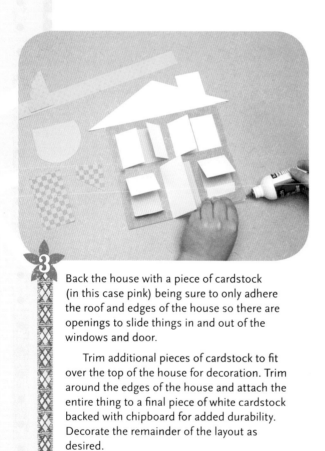

3 Back the house with a piece of cardstock (in this case pink) being sure to only adhere the roof and edges of the house so there are openings to slide things in and out of the windows and door.

Trim additional pieces of cardstock to fit over the top of the house for decoration. Trim around the edges of the house and attach the entire thing to a final piece of white cardstock backed with chipboard for added durability. Decorate the remainder of the layout as desired.

Crop photos and attach to paper-pieced people cut-outs to slide in windows and door frame.

Supplies: *Chipboard; handmade paper (Provo Craft); cardstock; woven accent (Hobby Lobby); animal clips (Pier 1); chalk ink; clear lacquer; bookbinding tape; adhesive foam*

The Jungle Comes Alive

Sometimes a flat layout just won't cut it. Some pictures just cry out for more dimensionality. So take a walk on the wild side and create a pop-up mini-book to display those photos that are just screaming for "more." The pop-up mechanism is simple to achieve. A simple accordion-folded piece of cardstock provides the base for the pages. Finish this adventurous book by simply cutting interestingly shaped windows out of the cardstock pages. Tuck your photos in and add a few hand-cut paper-pieced details, and you're all set! Welcome to the jungle!

ART CREATED BY TORREY SCOTT

Star Light, Star Bright

Catch this falling star and put it on your layout...never let it fade away. It looks very complex and impossible to re-create, but it's really not all that difficult. The covering for the star is a stamped image of a six-pointed star on cardstock then folded vertically down the middle. The internal structure of the star is made from a piece of patterned paper that has a large, repeating snowflake pattern on it. Trim a total of three snowflakes. Cut each snowflake in half and join each piece together with a valley-folded rectangle of transparency adhered along the cut edge between each section. Attach the two end snowflake halves—one to the background, one to the underside of the cover.

ART CREATED BY JEN LOWE

● ● ●

Supplies: *Cardstock; patterned paper (BasicGrey, Creative Imaginations); stamps (Stampendous, Stamps Happen); decorative punch (Emagination); metal snowflakes, snowflake stickers (Making Memories); snowflake brads (Creative Impressions); embossing powder; stamping ink; glitter glue; vellum*

Twinkle, twinkle,
find Jehovah's star?
Looking/seeing,
everywhere they are!

Snowflakes shining,
each one with six sides.
Star of David,
Oh! Where do you hide?

Wondering if
Jehovah's bright star
is inside all
the snowflakes there are.

Wonder always,
how He could design
in the heavens
this most perfect sign.

Believe, and see,
His artistic ways.
Fall down, worship,
all my live-long days.

The Star of David has 6 points, just like a snowflake. There are those who believe the Star of David is a sign that Jehovah will return to earth one day, and there are those who believe that each snowflake is on individual creation and design by God. And there are numerous unanswered questions as posed by this poem that I wrote a few years ago while watching huge snowflakes land on my hand and seeing the Star of David design in each flake. Snowflakes have beauty in the individuality of each flake. The Star of David has beauty in the wonder of faith, hope and belief. Can you find Jehovah's Star in each snowflake you see? I wonder if you can!!!

Supplies: *Patterned paper (Chatterbox); letter stickers (Chatterbox, Creative Imaginations); ribbon (BasicGrey); die-cut shape (Sizzix); Canadian font (Internet download)*

Family Fold

There are many other art forms that lend themselves well to scrapbooking. One of the most logical, but perhaps least obvious, is origami. After all, origami is all about the paper. The foundation for this unique pop-open tag book is based in this ancient art form. Believe it or not, it starts with a 12" x 12" (30cm x 30cm) square piece of paper that has been folded. See the steps on the next page for re-creating this heartwarming family album.

ART CREATED BY SAMANTHA WALKER

Flip It Tip

Give your projects some staying power! Here are some helpful tips on how to construct interactive features that won't fall apart.

Just say "No" to glue sticks! The glue turns brittle after a short period and will release. Instead, use permanent adhesive that's aggressive. ATG adhesives and heavy-duty glue like E6000 will give you the staying power you want.

Score it! Always score your paper before you fold it. This will help prevent breakage along the crease.

No wimpy stuff! Use heavy-weight cardstock whenever possible. Tag board, poster board, chipboard, or foamcore are very helpful in supporting your interactive features.

Cloth book binding tape It's a great way to add flexibility to hinged pieces and it's acid-free. Look for it online from book binding supply sites.

Lacquer it! Coating fragile elements in clear lacquer will make them more durable and shiny!

Bigger is better. Bigger, bolder, more substantial interactive pieces will hold up better in the long run. Delicate details won't make the long haul.

1 Start with double-sided square paper. Fold the paper diagonally corner to corner. Keeping the paper open to the same side, repeat folding on the other corner.

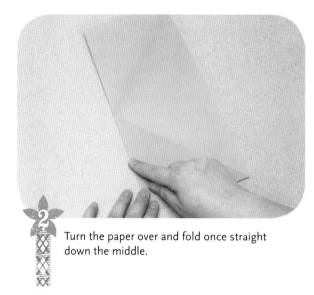

2 Turn the paper over and fold once straight down the middle.

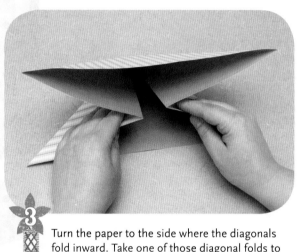
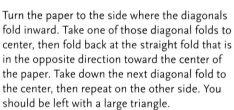

3 Turn the paper to the side where the diagonals fold inward. Take one of those diagonal folds to center, then fold back at the straight fold that is in the opposite direction toward the center of the paper. Take down the next diagonal fold to the center, then repeat on the other side. You should be left with a large triangle.

4 Using a straight-edge ruler and a craft knife, trim the triangle on both sides so you are left with a piece resembling a tag.

5 When opened, the tag should look like a plus sign. Discard the leftover square pieces or save for decorating the interior of the album. Repeat these steps for as many tags as you would like to create within your book.

6 Adhere the tags back to back to attach the entire book together.

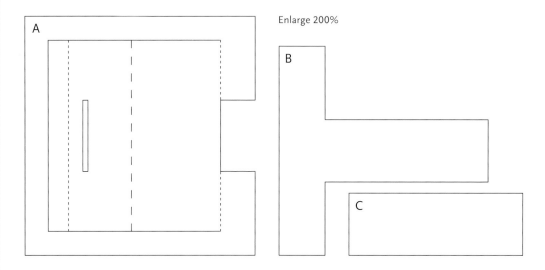

Enlarge 200%

Just the Two of Us template (page 60)

Trim and fold pieces A, B and C as shown.
Refer to page 61 for detailed assembly instructions.

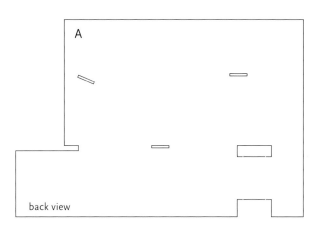

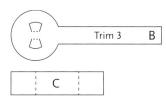

Enlarge 200%

Hazel & Harry moving paper doll template (page 62)

Trim all pieces from cardstock for durability. Trim pieces A and C and set aside. Trim three pieces of B; in each piece, trim two small tabs (cut on three sides only) and fold back. Position the three B pieces on the back of the layout (note: it is helpful to also position template A at this point as you'll have to be sure the extending B strips meet up with the slits in template A). Trim small holes in the layout and poke the cut-out tabs in B through the layout so they stick out on the front side. Adhere paper dolls to these tabs on the front of the layout. Slide the long strip portion of each of the B pieces through the corresponding slits in template A. Fold strip C and wrap it around template A as shown above. Apply adhesive to the underside of the folded C strip so that the template is permanently attached to the back of the layout but is able to slide back and forth easily.

Cut

Valley Fold

Mountain Fold

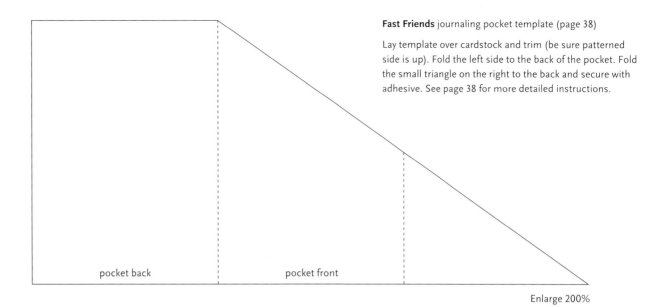

Fast Friends journaling pocket template (page 38)

Lay template over cardstock and trim (be sure patterned side is up). Fold the left side to the back of the pocket. Fold the small triangle on the right to the back and secure with adhesive. See page 38 for more detailed instructions.

pocket back

pocket front

Enlarge 200%

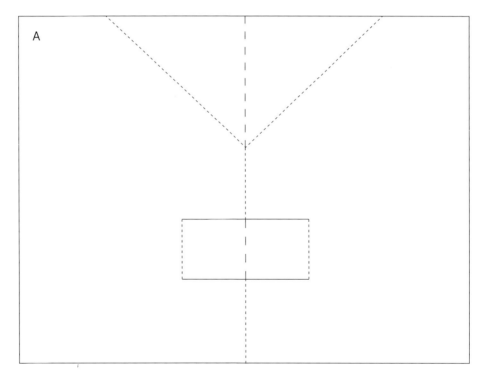

A

Always pop-up template (page 108)

Trim and fold along lines. Adhere piece B to the left side of the valley fold at the top of template A. Adhere piece C to left side of mountain fold cut from the bottom of template A. Add photos and other embellishments as desired.

Enlarge 200%

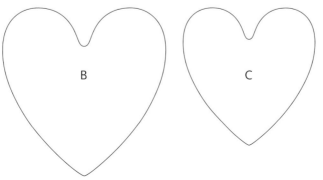

B

C

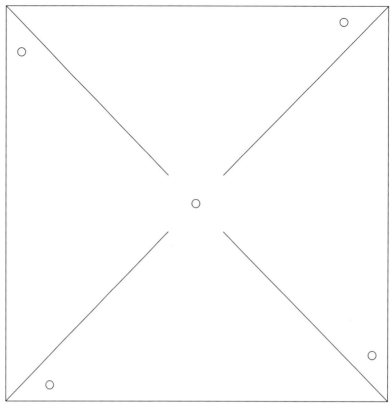

Enlarge 200%

Inner Beauty pinwheel template (page 86)

Lay the template over cardstock and trim along cut lines;
punch circles in corresponding holes. Fold the four pinwheel pieces
so the four points meet at the center and secure with a brad.
See page 87 for more detailed instructions.

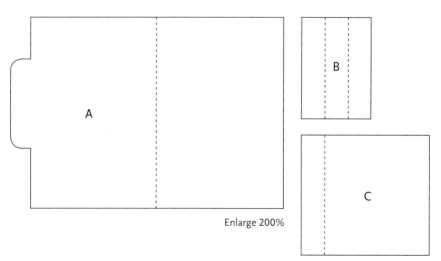

Enlarge 200%

Easter pop-up template (page 113)

Lay the templates over cardstock and trim. Fold along fold lines.
Adhere the right section of A to the layout background to construct
the flip-open file card. Adhere right outside section of B to right inside
section of A. Adhere left outside section of B to left outside section of
C. Adhere left outside section of C to left inside section of A.

Cut

- - - - - - -
Valley Fold

——— ———
Mountain Fold

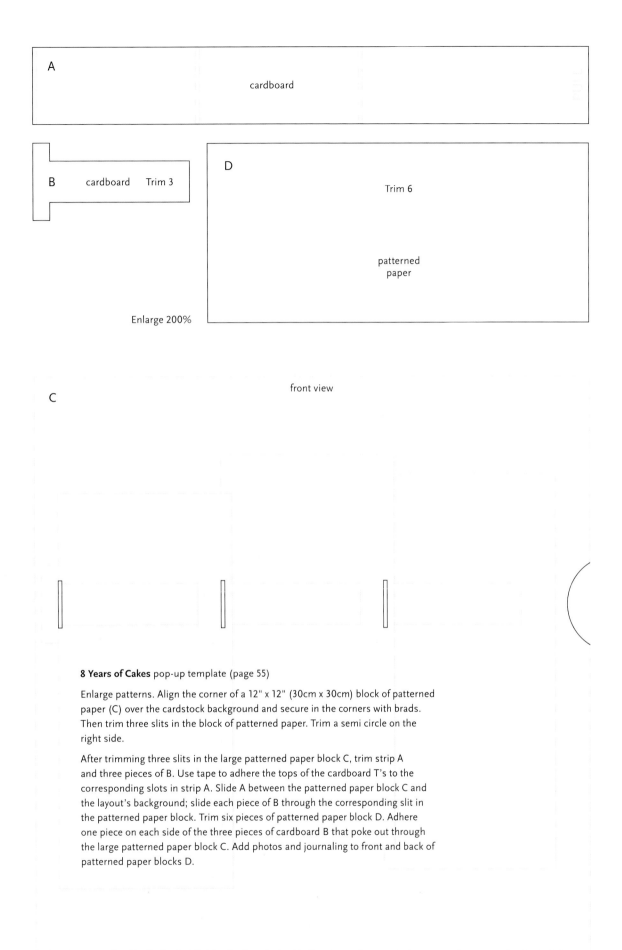

A

cardboard

B cardboard Trim 3

D

Trim 6

patterned
paper

Enlarge 200%

front view

C

8 Years of Cakes pop-up template (page 55)

Enlarge patterns. Align the corner of a 12" x 12" (30cm x 30cm) block of patterned paper (C) over the cardstock background and secure in the corners with brads. Then trim three slits in the block of patterned paper. Trim a semi circle on the right side.

After trimming three slits in the large patterned paper block C, trim strip A and three pieces of B. Use tape to adhere the tops of the cardboard T's to the corresponding slots in strip A. Slide A between the patterned paper block C and the layout's background; slide each piece of B through the corresponding slit in the patterned paper block. Trim six pieces of patterned paper block D. Adhere one piece on each side of the three pieces of cardboard B that poke out through the large patterned paper block C. Add photos and journaling to front and back of patterned paper blocks D.

Templates

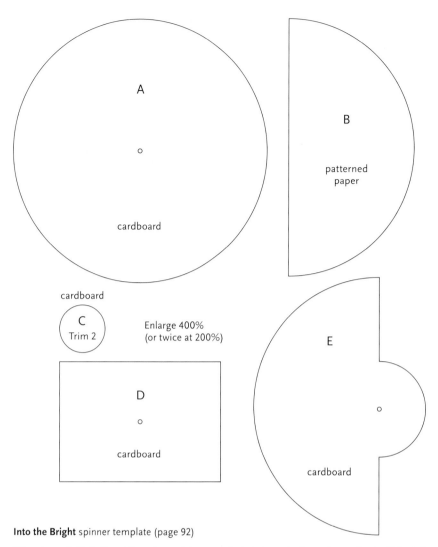

A
cardboard

o

B
patterned
paper

cardboard
C
Trim 2

Enlarge 400%
(or twice at 200%)

D
o
cardboard

E
o
cardboard

Into the Bright spinner template (page 92)

Trim pieces A, B, C, D and E as shown; trim a small circle in each piece where a brad will fit. Adhere journaling strips to the left side of A. Decorate B and E as desired. Adhere piece B to right side of A. Layer piece A/B, one C circle, piece E, the second C circle and piece D over the page background so the cut-out circles in the center align. Insert a large brad through all the pieces to allow for rotation. Add photo to top of piece D.

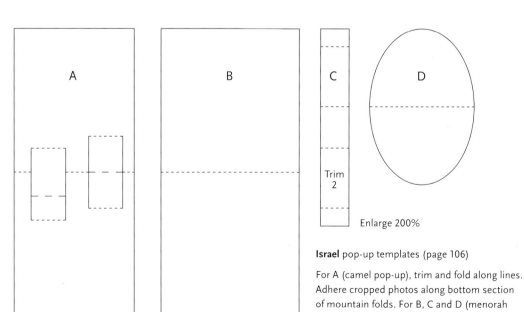

A

B

C

Trim
2

D

Enlarge 200%

Israel pop-up templates (page 106)

For A (camel pop-up), trim and fold along lines. Adhere cropped photos along bottom section of mountain folds. For B, C and D (menorah pop-up), trim and fold along lines. Accordion fold two strips of C and adhere these strips to B and D. Adhere stickers atop D.

Cut

- - - - - - -
Valley Fold

— — —
Mountain Fold

Source Guide

The following companies manufacture products featured in this book. Please check your local retailers to find these materials, or go to a company's Web site for the latest product. In addition, we have made every attempt to properly credit the items mentioned in this book. We apologize to any company that we have listed incorrectly, and we would appreciate hearing from you.

7gypsies
(877) 749-7797
www.sevengypsies.com

Adobe Systems Incorporated
(800) 833-6687
www.adobe.com

Adorn It / Carolee's Creations
(435) 563-1100
www.adornit.com

After Midnight Art Stamps
www.amstamps.com

All My Memories
(888) 553-1998
www.allmymemories.com

American Crafts
(801) 226-0747
www.americancrafts.com

American Traditional Designs
(800) 448-6656
www.americantraditional.com

ANW Crestwood
(973) 406-5000
www.anwcrestwood.com

Around The Block
(801) 593-1946
www.aroundtheblockproducts.com

Autumn Leaves
(800) 588-6707
www.autumnleaves.com

B Line Designs, LLC
(405) 376-3351
www.blinedesigns.com

BAM POP LLC
www.bampop.com

BasicGrey
(801) 544-1116
www.basicgrey.com

Bazzill Basics Paper
(480) 558-8557
www.bazzillbasics.com

Berwick Offray, LLC
(800) 344-5533
www.offray.com

Bo-Bunny Press
(801) 771-4010
www.bobunny.com

Buttons Galore & More
(856) 753-6700
www.buttonsgaloreandmore.com

C & T Publishing
(800) 284-1114
www.ctpub.com

ChartPak
(800) 628-1910
www.chartpak.com

Chatterbox, Inc.
(888) 416-6260
www.chatterboxinc.com

CherryArte
(212) 465-3495
www.cherryarte.com

Christine Adolf Designs
www.christineadolf.com

Cloud 9 Design
(866) 348-5661
www.cloud9design.biz

Collage Press
(435) 676-2039
www.collagepress.com

Colorbök, Inc.
(800) 366-4660
www.colorbok.com

Crafter's Workshop, The
(877) 272-3837
www.thecraftersworkshop.com

Crafty Secrets Publications
(888) 597-8898
www.craftysecrets.com

Crate Paper
(801) 798-8996
www.cratepaper.com

Creative Crystal Co.
(800) 578-0716
www.creative-crystal.com

Creative Imaginations
(800) 942-6487
www.cigift.com

Creative Impressions Rubber Stamps, Inc.
(719) 596-4860
www.creativeimpressions.com

Creative Memories
(800) 468-9335
www.creativememories.com

Crossed Paths
(972) 393-3755
www.crossedpaths.net

Daisy Bucket Designs
(541) 289-3299
www.daisybucketdesigns.com

Daisy D's Paper Company
(888) 601-8955
www.daisydspaper.com

Darice, Inc.
(800) 321-1494
www.darice.com

Design Originals
(800) 877-0067
www.d-originals.com

Designer Digitals
www.designerdigitals.com

Die Cuts With A View
(801) 224-6766
www.diecutswithaview.com

Doodlebug Design Inc.
(877) 800-9190
www.doodlebug.ws

Dream Street Papers
(480) 275-9736
www.dreamstreetpapers.com

Dymo
(800) 426-7827
www.dymo.com

EK Success, Ltd.
(800) 524-1349
www.eksuccess.com

Emagination Crafts, Inc.
(866) 238-9770
www.emaginationcrafts.com

Endless Gizy
no source available

Eyelet Outlet
(618) 622-9741
www.eyeletoutlet.com

Fancy Pants Designs, LLC
(801) 779-3212
www.fancypantsdesigns.com

Fiskars, Inc.
(866) 348-5661
www.fiskars.com

FontWerks
(604) 942-3105
www.fontwerks.com

Frances Meyer, Inc.
(413) 584-5446
www.francesmeyer.com

Grafix
(800) 447-2349
www.grafixarts.com

Hambly Studios
(800) 451-3999
www.hamblystudios.com

Heidi Grace Designs, Inc.
(866) 348-5661
www.heidigrace.com

Heidi Swapp / Advantus Corporation
(904) 482-0092
www.heidiswapp.com

Hero Arts Rubber Stamps, Inc.
(800) 822-4376
www.heroarts.com

Hobby Lobby Stores, Inc.
www.hobbylobby.com

Hot Off The Press, Inc.
(800) 227-9595
www.b2b.hotp.com

Imagination Project, Inc.
(888) 477-6532
www.imaginationproject.com

Jaquard Products / Rupert, Gibbon & Spider, Inc.
(800) 442-0455
www.jacquardproducts.com

Jen Lowe Designs
www.jenlowedesigns.com

Jesse James & Co., Inc.
(610) 435-0201
www.jessejamesbutton.com

Jo-Ann Stores
www.joann.com

JudiKins
(310) 515-1115
www.judikins.com

Judy's Stone House Designs
www.judysstonehousedesigns.com

Junkitz
(732) 792-1108
www.junkitz.com

K&Company
(888) 244-2083
www.kandcompany.com

Karen Burniston
www.karenburniston.com

Karen Foster Design
(801) 451-9779
www.karenfosterdesign.com

KI Memories
(972) 243-5595
www.kimemories.com

Krylon
(800) 457-9566
www.krylon.com

Lasting Impressions for Paper, Inc.
(800) 936-2677
www.lastingimpressions.com

Li'l Davis Designs
(480) 223-0080
www.lildavisdesigns.com

Making Memories
(801) 294-0430
www.makingmemories.com

Mark Richards Enterprises, Inc.
(888) 901-0091
www.markrichardsusa.com

May Arts
(800) 442-3950
www.mayarts.com

Maya Road, LLC
(214) 488-3279
www.mayaroad.com

me & my BiG ideas
(949) 583-2065
www.meandmybigideas.com

Melissa Frances / Heart & Home, Inc.
(888) 616-6166
www.melissafrances.com

Memories Complete, LLC
(866) 966-6365
www.memoriescomplete.com

Michaels Arts & Crafts
(800) 642-4235
www.michaels.com

Microsoft Corporation
www.microsoft.com

MOD — My Own Design
(303) 641-8680
www.mod-myowndesign.com

Mohawk Fine Papers, Inc.
www.mohawkpaper.com

Mrs. Grossman's Paper Company
(800) 429-4549
www.mrsgrossmans.com

My Mind's Eye, Inc.
(800) 665-5116
www.mymindseye.com

My Sentiments Exactly
(719) 260-6001
www.sentiments.com

Offray
see Berwick Offray, LLC

Paper Adventures
see ANW Crestwood

Paper Loft, The
(801) 254-1961
www.paperloft.com

Paper Studio
(480) 557-5700
www.paperstudio.com

Pebbles Inc.
(801) 235-1520
www.pebblesinc.com

Penny Black, Inc.
www.pennyblackinc.com

Pier 1 Imports
www.pier1.com

Pink Martini Designs
(845) 228-5833
www.pinkmartinidesigns.com

Plaid Enterprises, Inc.
(800) 842-4197
www.plaidonline.com

Prima Marketing, Inc.
(909) 627-5532
www.primamarketinginc.com

Provo Craft
(800) 937-7686
www.provocraft.com

PSX Design
www.sierra-enterprises.com/psxmain

Queen & Co.
(858) 613-7858
www.queenandcompany.com

QuicKutz, Inc.
(888) 702-1146
www.quickutz.com

Rhonna Designs
www.rhonnadesigns.com

Rouge de Garance
www.rougedegarance.com

Rusty Pickle
(801) 746-1045
www.rustypickle.com

Sakura Hobby Craft
(310) 212-7878
www.sakuracraft.com

Scenic Route Paper Co.
(801) 225-5754
www.scenicroutepaper.com

Scrapperdashery
www.scrapperdashery.com

Scrapworks, LLC / As You Wish Products, LLC
(801) 363-1010
www.scrapworks.com

SEI, Inc.
(800) 333-3279
www.shopsei.com

Shalom Scrapper
(925) 451-3529
www.shalomscrapper.com

Sizzix
(877) 355-4766
www.sizzix.com

Spellbinders Paper Arts, LLC
(888) 547-0400
www.spellbinders.us

Stampendous!
(800) 869-0474
www.stampendous.com

Stampers Anonymous
(800) 945-3980
www.stampersanonymous.com

Stamps Happen, Inc.
(800) 445-5565
www.stampshappen.com

Strano Designs
(508) 454-4615
www.stranodesigns.com

Strathmore Papers
(also see Mohawk Fine Papers)
(800) 628-8816
www.strathmore.com

Sugarloaf Products, Inc.
(770) 484-0722
www.sugarloafproducts.com

Sulyn Industries, Inc.
(954) 755-2511
www.sulyn.com

Technique Tuesday, LLC
(503) 644-4073
www.techniquetuesday.com

Times to Cherish
(800) 848-2848
www.timestocherish.com

Two Peas in a Bucket
(888) 896-7327
www.twopeasinabucket.com

Two Purple Pandas
(214) 634-1283
www.twopurplepandas.com

Urban Lily
www.urbanlily.com

Very Useful Paper Co., The
no source available

Wal-Mart Stores, Inc.
www.walmart.com

Wilton Industries
www.wilton.com

Wordsworth
(877) 280-0934
www.wordsworthstamps.com

WorldWin Papers
(888) 834-6455
www.worldwinpapers.com

Wrights Ribbon Accents
(877) 597-4448
www.wrights.com

Zsiage, LLC
(718) 224-1976
www.zsiage.com

Index

A

accordion-folded elements 37-38, 50, 58-59, 76, 110
archival-safe, tips for keeping layouts 27

B

beads 23
beeswax 31
buttons 12, 14-15, 24, 30, 50

C

cardstock, textured 11, 19, 22
closures/enclosures, list of 36
Contributing Artists 3

E

embossing 11, 26

F

fabric 15, 17-18, 24
felt 14
fibers 24
flip elements 66-68, 73-74, 76-77, 81, 83-85, 89, 93, 100, 112
Flip It Tips 13, 21, 27, 36, 51, 63, 77, 82, 95, 98, 109, 112, 118

G

glitter 25, 52

H

hand stitching 12-15, 24
hidden journaling 35-40, 44-45, 48, 51, 54-55, 58-60, 62, 66-68, 70, 72-74, 76-77, 82-84, 89-90, 92-93
hidden photos 34, 37, 40, 43, 45-46, 49-50, 54-55, 56, 80, 83, 85, 88, 93

I

interactivity, more ways to experiment with 51, 89, 95
Introduction 7

M

machine stitching 18, 23
memorabilia 13, 42
metal accents 16, 19, 26-27, 31, 36
mini albums 25, 38, 43, 51, 59, 81, 84, 102, 106, 109-111, 116
mountain fold 98

P

paper engineering, books on 63
Passion for Pop-Ups, A 96-119
plastic texture sheet 28-29
pop-up elements 98-119
price tags 39
pull elements 34-52, 54-56, 58, 60, 62-63

R

rhinestones 25
ribbon 18, 20, 25, 27, 30, 34

S

scalloped edges 18, 42, 98
shaker elements 75
silk flowers 10, 34, 52
Skinny on Flipping & Spinning, The 64-95
slide elements 34-36, 38-49, 51-52, 56, 59, 60, 62-63
Source Guide 125-126
spin elements 69-72, 78, 80, 82, 86, 88, 90, 92, 94
stability, tips for 118
step-by-step instructions 13, 21, 29, 38, 46, 53, 57, 61, 72, 79, 87, 91, 95, 102, 104, 110, 115, 119

T

Table of Contents 5
Templates 120-124
texture 10-31
To Slide or Not to Slide 32-63
Touchable Textures 8-31
tulle 12-13

V

valley fold 98

W

wall art 30

Discover More Ways to Stretch Your Artistic Imagination with Memory Makers Books!

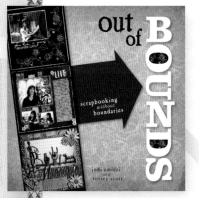

Out of Bounds

Push the boundaries of your scrapbooking with creative inspiration and innovative ideas from leading scrapbook designers Jodi Amidei and Torrey Scott.

ISBN-13: 978-1-59963-009-0
ISBN-10: 1-59963-009-5

paperback
128 pages
Z0795

Tantalizing Textures

Learn from scrapbook artist Trudy Sigurdson ways to infuse textural themes from photographs into scrapbook art using textiles, metals, natural elements, art mediums, paper and clear elements.

ISBN-13: 978-1-59963-005-2
ISBN-10: 1-59963-005-2

paperback
128 pages
Z0715

Ask the Masters!
Making the Most of Your Scrapbook Supplies

Innovative and inspiring ideas from the Memory Makers Masters for using that growing stash of scrapbook supplies and tools.

ISBN-13: 978-1-59963-012-0
ISBN-10: 1-59963-012-5

paperback
128 pages
Z1040

These books and other fine Memory Makers Titles are available at your local scrapbook or craft store, bookstore or from online suppliers, including www.memorymakersmagazine.com and www.fwbookstore.com.